Using Data for Monitoring and Target Setting

Using Data for Monitoring and Target Setting is a clear and practical guide for teachers and school administrative staff that shows how to use spreadsheets to create orderly records of assessment. These can then be used for the sort of statistical analyses which are now being demanded.

This guide includes

- lots of practical examples
- step-by-step instructions on how to obtain the data you want
- simple advice on how to use Excel
- pictures of the actual screens you will be using.

No prior experience is necessary. Even the most technophobic teacher will find this easy to follow, but the experienced manager will also have something to learn. The techniques covered will be complementary to the data now required by the LEAs, DfEE and school governors.

Ray Sumner has worked in education for many years, both as a teacher and a researcher. He is the author of *The Role of Assessment in Schools*.
Ian McCallum taught mathematics before going on to work at the London Research Centre, where he analysed a wide variety of educational data.

Using Data for Monitoring and Target Setting

A Practical Guide for Teachers

RAY SUMNER
and
IAN McCALLUM

London and New York

First published 1999
by Routledge
11 New Fetter Lane, London EC4P 4EE

Simultaneously published in the USA and Canada
by Routledge
29 West 35th Street, New York, NY 10001

© 1999 Ray Sumner and Ian McCallum
Reprinted 1999
Routledge is an imprint of Taylor & Francis Group

Typeset in Sabon by Solidus (Bristol) Limited
Printed in Great Britain by
Unwin Brothers Limited, Old Woking, Surrey

British Library Cataloguing in Publication Data
A catalogue record for this book is available from the British Library

Library of Congress Cataloging in Publication Data
Sumner, Raymond.
Using data for monitoring and target setting : a practical guide
for teachers / Ray Sumner, Raymond
p. cm.
Includes bibliographical reference and index.
1. Educational tests and measurements—Great Britain—Data
processing—Handbooks, manuals, etc. I. McCallum, Ian, 1931– .
II. Title
LB3056.G7S86 1999 98–30838
371.26'0941—dc21 CIP

ISBN 0–415–19686–8

Contents

What You Need to Use This Handbook

You need a PC with Excel Version 7 and WORD Version 7 (or Versions 2 and 4, respectively).

Aims of the Handbook

PRESSURES ON SCHOOLS AND GOOD PRACTICE

Schools are obliged by law to set targets vetted by the local education authority (LEA) to ensure that they are sufficiently ambitious. Publication adds pressure to meet ever higher expectations. The crude standard assessment tasks (SATs), General Certificate of Secondary Education (GCSE) and A level tables and the many LEA systems for 'value added' analyses all provide for comparisons between schools. Some schemes take into account circumstances related to pupils' school and test performance, so to an extent are 'fairer'. The questions that schools are called on to answer are *How well have the pupils done by the end of a Key Stage?* and *Have the pupils made the progress they ought?* It is obvious to us that conscientious teachers and well-run schools have always asked these questions. Both are difficult to answer, especially with limited means for organising and analysing the varied data which may be of relevance.

Effective schools use a variety of methods for monitoring pupils' attainments. Most rely on teachers' assessments; many use standardised measures to gauge pupils' abilities or other attributes, particularly for special needs diagnosis and guidance on course choice. Good practice, we believe, goes beyond using these assessments for individual pupils; it extends to looking critically at group progress, in order to aid curriculum review, teaching and school development. Data collected for the LEA scheme might be of use to schools for their own purposes, which may well complement the government's and the LEA's. But schools should have a sound basis to set targets which satisfy governors, heads and teachers as to their validity. Without the capacity to carry out their own analyses, schools inevitably relinquish a degree of control. The Handbook aims to enhance this capacity.

OBJECTIVES OF THE HANDBOOK

1   To introduce the reader to data handling in Excel via a series of staged exercises.
2   To show teachers and support staff how to use computing techniques to organise the data they have and to conduct relevant statistical analyses.

3 To provide ready access to explanations of the statistical methods by the use of, in most cases, actual pupil and school data. We expect users to develop understanding of the methods and to acquire insights into applications for their own schools.

4 To give teachers the confidence to try various statistical methods as aids for enhancing their own work with pupils and to be impartial when evaluating analyses conducted by outside agencies.

5 To help schools to carry out analyses of data for their own purposes, principally in support of pupils' attainments. Also to indicate how analyses can be used in school evaluation and to fulfil the legal obligations to set school targets annually.

WHAT YOU WILL BE ABLE TO DO

When you have worked through the examples, you will be able to

- accumulate data from assessments and other sources in well-ordered files to derive more meaning from the data as they accumulate
- conduct accurate analyses of selected variables
- choose the analyses best suited to your purposes
- appreciate the basis for the statistics you calculate
- interpret the statistics in the light of your knowledge of the pupils, school characteristics and feedback from LEA or national systems
- review the progress of individual pupils and discuss targets with them
- appraise particular factors which may affect aspects of pupil attainment and school effectiveness
- engage in setting feasible whole school targets
- present information to parents, governors and teachers which is informative and accurate.

TARGETS, MONITORING AND ASSESSMENT

We perceive that a culture change is being forced on schools. Customarily, assessment was seen by teachers as focused on the pupil's learning as mediated by the teacher. Admittedly, external policies intervened at certain points in time; for transfer and selection, allocation of LEA resources, identification of special educational needs (SEN) pupils, accreditation and accountability. But internal policies were more central, such as to give feedback to pupils on their learning (attainments), diagnose pupils' learning problems, pinpoint specific difficulties, group pupils for teaching, provide guidance on course choice and study methods, and evaluate curricula for improvement. Our concern is that sound internal policies should not be abandoned in order to service the external demands.

Our belief is that both sets of policies can be met by using computing facilities to make selective use of assessment data. Schemes for departments or years should identify those assessments which enable the periodic monitoring of attainments. The marks or grades for these should all be recorded on computer file(s). Certain additional assessments may be crucial, unless tests provided by the LEA are apt, such as of reasoning ability, language skills, etc. Also, whenever possible, each pupil's previous Key Stage (KS) level(s) should be recorded. By working in this way, schools will have data available for a range of (monitoring) procedures for appraising year groups or departments, classes within years, and individuals. Targets for external use should draw on the pool of information from monitoring analyses.

Examples of questions you might answer by using the methods we outline are

- How do we keep pupils' assessment records on computer file to be able to get more meaning from the data as they accumulate?
- Can we summarise measures accurately for ease of understanding?
- When are predictions of pupil 'success or failure' justified?
- What would we accept as evidence that the school has been effective?
- How should we evaluate the targets for the school proposed by the LEA?
- What particular circumstances would the governors recognise as influencing the standards achieved by the pupils?
- How may the school management team (SMT) and governors make progress checks each year?

Recent publications have confirmed our view that targets should be based upon systematic monitoring carried out at various stages as each cohort progresses through school. A particular difficulty is the change within a cohort as some pupils leave and others join. For example, a group of 56 pupils in Year 3 had 58 by Year 6 but included only 31 of the original group. Consequently, about 60 per cent of the pupils were included in the evaluation of attainment in relation to 'abilities' and KS2 levels. Two ways for dealing with this problem are first, to accumulate data year by year and occasionally aggregate them for comparable groups, and second, to give intermediate assessments when the interval between earlier and later results is more than 18 months to 2 years.

The descriptive statistics produced by monitoring will inevitably reveal the variability inherent in measures of attainment and abilities. For instance, when two successive Year 7 groups obtained similar means of about 102 on a reading test but percentages of 67 and 72 at level 6 or higher for English, what might be amiss? In fact, the difference could quite properly be ascribed to natural variation. But, regrettably, schools are likely *to seek explanations where none are required*. We show, by looking at the probable extent of variability why this is the case. As forecasting entails relatively even more variation, we indicate how targets should be pitched within defined limits. However, rather than set out a model for schools to follow, we have described established methods which could suit various school contexts.

Some of the questions we suggested above can best be answered by summarising pupil's performance assessments. Here, schools should aim for consistency year by year and, provided the curriculum does not alter greatly, could use the same assessment schemes and even tasks or questions with successive cohorts. We have illustrated how circumstances may influence pupil (school) performance, so individual data (e.g. free school meals, English as additional language, level of SEN, sex) may be analysed too. Also attainment may be appraised in terms of school conditions (e.g. pupil–teacher ratios, absence rates, official and unofficial funding levels, proportions of pupils on SEN register, exclusion rates). We think that schools who do not have computerised records should develop this facility and then produce descriptive statistics for classes and year-groups. From these they can derive others, such as 'rolling means', to examine trends. Later on they will wish to investigate aspects they might influence by changing the opportunities in the school (curricula, options, SEN provision, homework clubs, etc.) and so revise targets. There is so much diversity between schools that while inter-school comparisons may produce useful indicators, such as value added indices, internal evaluation grounded on sound data collection and analysis is the key to understanding effectiveness and improvement.

HOW THE HANDBOOK IS ORGANISED

Part 1 is concerned with using Excel for data handling and computing indices and other statistics. Limited explanations of some statistics are given but the emphasis is on getting the results required on to the screen. In Part 2A, we explain the basis of various types of scales that may be used in schools, mentioning the good and bad points of some. This section should be especially helpful to teachers who have made little use of tests but may wish to consider them for a monitoring scheme. Part 2B gives further explanation of certain statistics and their applications in monitoring and setting targets for groups and individual pupils.

Part 1
First Steps with Excel

This section uses practical examples with a school's data to show you how to perform everyday operations. If you already know basic procedures, you may wish to proceed immediately to the next section. We assume that, having loaded Excel, you are presented with a worksheet as part of the screen that looks like the one shown in Screen 1.

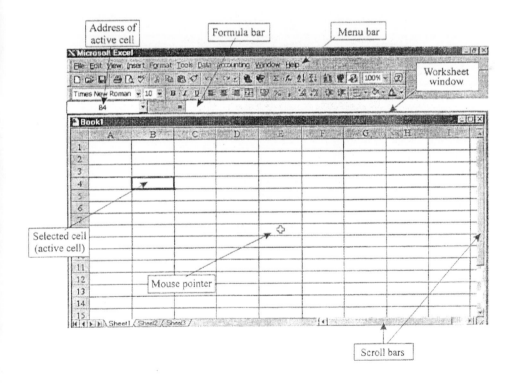

Screen 1

The 'mouse pointer' follows the movements made with the mouse on your desk. To enter a letter or number in a cell, first use the mouse to move the pointer to the chosen cell and press ('click') the left mouse key to make it the active cell. Any character entered on the keyboard and followed by the 'enter' key is then retained in that cell.

When you wish to access a part of the worksheet outside the area of the worksheet window, move the pointer onto a scroll bar where it changes to an arrow. Next, click and hold down the left mouse key and move the scroll bar until the required part of the worksheet is displayed; then release the mouse key.

After typing a figure (or letter) press the 'Enter' key, or ↵ key symbol, and the pointer will automatically move to the cell below, ready for your next entry in a column. You can enter a row of figures (or letters) by using the tab key [⇆] instead of the enter key, when the pointer will move to the next cell in the row.

ENTERING PUPIL RECORDS

It is usually convenient to enter each pupil's record as a complete row, then move to the next row for the next pupil, to create a table as in Table 1. If you do not have similar data, you should enter the class record provided in Appendix 1 (part of which is reproduced in Table 1) for the exercises which follow.

Table 1 Sample data for the boys in two Year 2 classes (Pupil performance on Writing Test/Task)

Surname	First name	Sex	Nurs	FSM	Write T/T		Maths T/T		ScSubLvl
Adams	John	b	Yes	Yes	2C		2C		2
Andrews	Geoffrey	b	Yes	No	2B		2A		3
Bennet	Peter	b	Yes	No		3		3	3
Bowen	Peter	b	Yes	No		3		3	3
Brain	Richard	b	Yes	No	2C		2A		3
Brown	John	b	Yes	No	2C		2B		2
Burton	Alistair	b	Yes	No	2B			3	3
Burton	Reg	b	No	No		3		3	3
Cane	Sean	b	Yes	No	2C		2A		3
Clegg	Oliver	b	Yes	No	2B			3	3
Collin	David	b	Yes	No	2C		2C		2
Curtis	Harold	b	Yes	No		2	2C		2
Dunne	William	b	Yes	No	2B		2A		2
English	Leonard	b	Yes	No	2A		2B		3
French	Ian	b	Yes	No		3		3	3
Godfrey	Sam	b	Yes	No		2	2C		2
Green	John	b	Yes	No	2B			3	3
Hall	Wain	b	Yes	No	2C		2C		1
Howard	Arthur	b	No	Yes	2C		2B		2
Howe	Gordon	b	Yes	Yes	2C		2C		2
Jones	Andrew	b	No	No	2B			3	3
Katlin	Earnest	b	Yes	No	2C		2B		2
Macrae	Neil	b	Yes	No		2		2	1
Noble	Dennis	b	No	No	2C		2B		2

Reed	Stephen	b	No	Yes	2B	2A		2
Spencer	Ian	b	No	No	2C		2	2
Staples	Seamus	b	Yes	No	2C	2C		2
Street	Neil	b	No	No		3	3	3
Thorpe	Alan	b	Yes	No	2B	2B		3
Vernon	Charles	b	No	No	2B	2A		3
Ward	Roger	b	Yes	No	2A		3	3
Weston	Colin	b	No	No	2B		3	3
White	Gerald	b	Yes	No	2C	2A		3
Wood	Donald	b	Yes	No	2A		3	3

(The complete data for boys and girls are included in Appendix 1)

Key	Nurs	attended nursery provision
	FSM	has free school meals
	WriteT/T	Key Stage 1 Test or Task level attained in writing
	MathsT/T	Key Stage 1 Test or Task level attained in maths
	ScSubLvl	Key Stage subject level attained in science

Our example uses actual Key Stage 1 results from 68 children in two classes in one school (the names are fictitious). You can use these, or similar data of your own, for the following exercise. Data for boys have been included on p. 16 and complete data, for boys and girls, are provided in Appendix 1.

To create your table in Excel, move the pointer to cell A1, click and hold the left key down while you move the pointer first to column H and then down until you reach row 69 or beyond, and release the key. You have now selected a block of cells, which appear dark, into which you can enter your records in a systematic manner. Cell A1 appears white and is the 'active cell' ready for your first entry.

You can use the Key Stage 1 results provided in Table 1.

Cell A1 is now the active cell on your screen and, if you wish to use the data provided, enter 'Surname' and press the tab key [⇥]. Continue entering the remaining headings (each one followed by [⇥]) until all the headings have been entered when the active cell moves automatically to the first cell in the second row (A2) ready for the name 'Adams'. Screen 2 shows the first few entries, with the active cell in position E7, ready for the next entry. Column F, for Writing Test/Task, shows how the program aligns numbers to the right and text to the left.

When you have entered some or all of the records, it is important that you save them.

SAVING YOUR WORK

It is good practice to save your information, and you will probably want to do this on a $3^1/_2$ inch floppy disk. To do so (having made sure that you have a disk in your floppy disk drive) move the pointer to 'File' in the menu bar, then click (briefly press down the left mouse key) to produce a drop down menu, on which you move the mouse pointer to 'Save As . . .' and click again. Your screen will look similar to that shown in Screen 3.

If '$3^1/_2$ Floppy (A:)' does not appear alongside 'Save in:' click on the small ▾ to see the alternative drives on which your data can be saved and then click on '$3^1/_2$ Floppy (A:)' unless you wish to save it elsewhere. (You may choose to save it on your hard

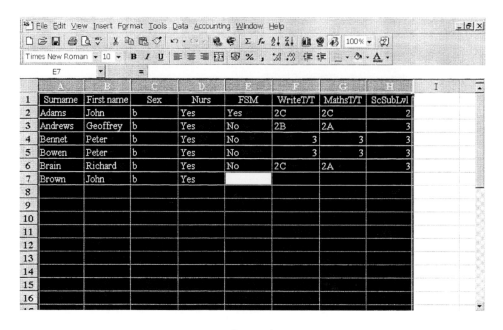

Screen 2

Screen 3

disk – usually drive C.) In this example the file was given the name KS197.xls before clicking on '$\underline{S}$ave'.

Whenever you amend your records, you will need to save the latest version. You can do this merely by clicking on [$\underline{F}$ile] then [$\underline{S}$ave] and your original file will be replaced by the amended version.

SOME BASIC OPERATIONS

Although entering records in the form shown may be convenient, it is usually easier to work with numbers rather than letters. Your next task, which is to convert the levels 2A, 2B, 2C etc. to numbers, should take only a minute or so.

When assigning letters to indicate levels of attainment, we usually assume that B is as much better than C as A is better than B and we might view numerical marks in a similar way. For this exercise the table has been used to convert Key Stage levels to numerical marks.

Level	W	1	2C	2B	2A	3
Numeric code	1.5	2	2.25	2.5	2.75	3

The new values imply that the differences between levels 'W' (working towards), '1', '2B' and '3' are all equal. A good case could be made for using different values (e.g. W – 0.5, 1 – 1.5, 2B – 2.5, and 3 – 3.5; i.e. each level with a range of attainments with 0.5 located at the mid-point) and you may wish to explore the effect such changes would have in later calculations. (Some LEAs or agencies use level ordinal numbers as scale values, with W=0 etc. These are simpler to understand but less valid conceptually than our proposed scales.)

Finding and Replacing Values

We shall start by changing the letters b and g to the numeric values 1 and 2 so that each boy is indicated by 1 and each girl by 2.

First, highlight column C ('Sex') by clicking on the column label 'C'. (Alternatively you could use the mouse to click on one cell and then, while holding down the left mouse key, drag the pointer to highlight the selected area.) Now use the mouse to select [Edit] then [Replace] and you will be presented with a screen that is similar to Screen 4.

Type 'b' under 'Find what', press the tab key and type '1' under 'Replace with:' as

Screen 4

in Screeen 4. It is a sensible precaution to click the box 'Find entire cells <u>o</u>nly' before clicking on 'Replace <u>A</u>ll'. (You could use '<u>F</u>ind Next' and 'R<u>e</u>place' to change single values if you prefer to be more cautious.) After replacing 'b' with '1' repeat the procedure to replace 'g' with '2' so that all the girls are identified with the number 2.

Highlight columns D and E together and replace 'Yes' with '1' and 'No' with '2' and then highlight columns F and G and replace level '2A' with 2.75; 2B with 2.5 etc.

As a precaution, in order to preserve your initial records, you may wish to save your revised work under a different name (e.g. KS197v2.XLS).

Basic Statistics

A widely used statistical measure is 'Average'; strictly speaking this is the 'arithmetic mean' because it is obtained by dividing the sum of a series of values by the number in the series (see Part 2A, pp. 43–5).

We shall now calculate the mean for the Writing Test/Task values assigned to pupils in our data. *If you have these figures on 3¹/₂ disk, in your drive, you can obtain them directly by clicking on* [<u>F</u>ile] *then* [<u>O</u>pen] *and* KS197v2.XLS. Remember, if '3¹/₂ Floppy (A:)' does not appear alongside 'Look <u>i</u>n:' use the mouse to click on the small ▾ to see the alternative disk drives from which your data can be obtained and then click on '3¹/₂ Floppy (A:)'.

Part of your Excel screen should appear as in Screen 5.

	A	B	C	D	E	F	G	H
1	Surname	First name	Sex	Nurs	FSM	WriteT/T	MathsT/T	ScSubLvl
2	Adams	John	1	1	1	2.25	2.25	2
3	Andrews	Geoffrey	1	1	2	2.5	2.75	3
4	Bennet	Peter	1	1	2	3	3	3
5	Bowen	Peter	1	1	2	3	3	3
6	Brain	Richard	1	1	2	2.25	2.75	3
7	Brown	John	1	1	2	2.25	2.5	2
8	Burton	Alistair	1	1	2	2.5	3	3
9	Burton	Reg	1	2	2	3	3	3
10	Cane	Sean	1	1	2	2.25	2.75	3
11	Clegg	Oliver	1	1	2	2.5	3	3
12	Collin	David	1	1	2	2.25	2.25	2
13	Curtis	Harold	1	1	2	2	2.25	2
14	Dunne	William	1	1	2	2.5	2.75	2
15	English	Leonard	1	1	2	2.75	2.5	3
16	French	Ian	1	1	2	3	3	3

Screen 5

Excel will calculate for you the average of any variable (column of figures) you choose. To do this, click on an empty cell, where you wish your 'average' to appear, and type =Average(and immediately move the pointer to the first value in the column, i.e. cell F2 headed WriteT/T and, while keeping the left mouse key depressed, drag the pointer to the foot of the column (cell F69). Your formula will now appear as =Average(F2:F69. You must now enter the second bracket (immediately after the 9), press the Enter key and you will be provided with the average (2.481618) of all the Writing Test/Task scores. (*Hint*: it is sometimes more convenient to highlight a block of cells by clicking on the first cell and then moving to the last cell in the block and holding down one of the shift keys as you click in the last cell. The whole block of cells will then be highlighted.)

Some Simple Checks and Other Basic Statistics

No method of checking the accuracy of data can replace the conventional, labour-intensive, methods. However, a proportion of data entry errors can lead to figures that are excessively large or small and a check can be made for these by finding maximum and minimum values in your data. *Note: blank cells are ignored and not included in calculations. This is not the same as having a value of zero.*

Use the same method as before to make the following entries to cells F70, F71 and F72.

=MIN(F2:F69)
=AVERAGE(F2:F69)
=MAX(F2:F69)

To give you

2
2.481618
3

There is no need to work to the six decimal places provided and, after highlighting the relevant cells, the number of places can be reduced by using the mouse to select [Format] [Cells] [Number] [Number] and then the number of decimal places required (in this case 2). When you've done this, your data will look like this:

2.00
2.48
3.00

Saving Labour by Copying, Cutting and Pasting

You can avoid re-entering the formulae under each column for which we require the statistical information by copying the formulae already entered to the corresponding positions in other columns. This is achieved as follows: use the mouse to highlight the three formulae (F70:F72) before clicking on [Edit] [Copy]. Now move the mouse pointer to cell G70 and click on [Edit] [Paste] and the three formulae will have been pasted into cells G70, G71 and G72. The formulae have been automatically changed to work on the next column (G) and have now become:

=MIN(G2:G69)	2.00
=AVERAGE(G2:G69)	2.69
=MAX(G2:G69)	3.00

> *Tip*: to copy and paste more efficiently hold down the control [Control] and [C] keys together to copy and then, having moved the mouse pointer to the required cell, paste by holding down the [Control] and [V] keys together.

You can copy the three cells F70:F72 into the next two columns in one step by highlighting and copying the three cells and then, after highlighting the cells (G70:H70) as shown in Screen 6, pasting them into columns G and H.

	A	B	C	D	E	F	G	H	I
68	Wortley	Beryl	2	1	2	2.25	2.5	2	
69	Young	Megan	2	1	2	2.75	3	3	
70						2.00			
71						2.48			
72						3.00			

Tip: it is convenient to be able to see the column headings when working lower down on the worksheet. Move the mouse pointer to the position shown and then hold down the left key and drag the bar down the screen.

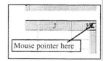

Mouse pointer here

Screen 6

Your worksheet can now be divided into two windows, one of which can still show the first few rows which include the column headings as shown in Screen 7.

	A	B	C	D	E	F	G	H	I	J	K
1	Surname	First name	Sex	Nurs	FSM	WriteT/T	MathsT/T	ScSubLvl			
2	Adams	John	1	1	1	2.25	2.25	2			
69	Young	Megan	2	1	2	2.75	3	3			
70				Minimum		2.00	2.00	1.00			
71				Average		2.48	2.67	2.47			
72				Maximum		3.00	3.00	3.00			
73											

Screen 7

It is useful to include labels. In this example 'Minimum', 'Average' and 'Maximum' have been typed into cells D70, D71 and D72.

Placing Answers Where They Are Needed

You could, of course, have entered your formulae in any suitable cell but, for this exercise, it seemed sensible to place the first results at the foot of each relevant column of figures. It is often more convenient to place them in some other location. This can be achieved by highlighting the cells that you wish to move and then cutting them [Edit] [Cut] before moving the mouse pointer to the new location and pasting them [Edit] [Paste].

If you try this and then click on the cells at the new location, you will see that the formulae still apply to the correct cells and your answers are therefore unchanged.

Calculating the Sum of a Column of Figures

You can calculate the sum of a group of figures with the formula =SUM(F2:F69) typed in any empty cell. (Note: as with other formulae, the array of cells with figures that are to be summed can include more than one column.)

An easier method of summing figures is to move the pointer to the cell where the total is to be placed and click the left key to make this the active cell. Now click on the symbol Σ (just below the menu bar) when the formula will be instantly inserted in the active cell. Sometimes Excel will 'guess' which figures are to be summed. If it doesn't, or selects the wrong cells, you need only to highlight the correct cells before pressing the 'Enter' key.

Changing the Order of Records (Sorting)

In our example, pupil records are in alphabetical order of surname with boys first and then girls. You might wish to change this to rank order by achievement in the Writing Test/Task. To achieve this, highlight the whole table including all the names and marks (also include the headings). Then use the mouse to select [Data] [Sort] when you will be presented with Screen 8.

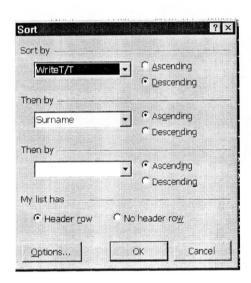

By clicking on the small ▼ you are presented with the headings of the columns which can be used to sort your records. In this case we have selected the Write Test/Task result for our first sort to be followed by the Surname for those with equal marks.

Note: 'Descending' has been checked for the test results and we have indicated that a header row (not to be sorted) has been included.

Screen 8

If you have made a mistake you can use [Edit] [Undo sort] to restore the list to its original order.

The first part of your list should now look like Table 2 on page 14.

Recording the Rank Order

You might wish to restore your records to the original order but keep a record of the ranks of each of the pupils. With a small number of records this can be achieved by entering the rank order in a new column. We could, for example, enter 1 in cell I2, 2 in I3 and so on until we reached 68 in cell I69. You will have noticed that this would

Table 2

Surname	First name	Sex	Nurs	FSM	Write T/T	Maths T/T	ScSubLvl
Bennet	Peter	1	1	2	3	3	3
Bowen	Peter	1	1	2	3	3	3
Burton	Reg	1	2	2	3	3	3
Courtney	Mary	2	1	2	3	3	3
French	Ian	1	1	2	3	3	3
Street	Neil	1	2	2	3	3	3
Webb	Susan	2	1	2	3	3	3
Weeks	Hazel	2	1	2	3	3	3
Whelan	Wendy	2	1	2	3	2.75	3
Crick	Susan	2	1	2	2.75	2.75	3
English	Leonard	1	1	2	2.75	2.5	3
Macrae	Jean	2	1	2	2.75	2.75	2
Saggers	June	2	1	2	2.75	2.75	3
Tennison	Alison	2	1	2	2.75	2.5	3

not be fair to pupils with the same mark whose rank was decided by the order of their surname. (Thus Peter Bennet would gain the top rank of 1 and Hazel Weeks, with an identical score, would be ranked eighth.) You should therefore adjust your ranks to take account of any ties (see also Part 2A, p. 44).

You could use Excel to rank scores more efficiently in the following way. Having placed the results in rank order, choose the column in which you want the ranks to appear and enter 1 against the pupil with the highest rank.

Let us assume that the ranks are in column I. In the cell immediately below the '1' that you have just entered, type = I2+1. Now copy this cell and paste it down into all the cells in which you require a rank to appear.

> *Tip:* If you wish to insert a column, perhaps immediately after 'MathsT/T' (a new column H) you merely highlight the whole of column H (by clicking on the letter H) and then select – [Insert] [Columns]

You will see that you now have a column that shows the rank order of every pupil. At this stage you could deal with tied ranks. Our example has too many tied ranks to justify producing rank orders but if only two had tied for first place, you could replace the second rank '2' label with a 1 and the following rank with the figure 3 and subsequent ranks would be changed automatically. You would then have to look for other ties and deal with them similarly.

When you are satisfied that all the ranks are correct you must remove all your formulae. You can achieve this by copying the column but, before pasting it into the same position, click on [Edit] [Paste Special] [Values] to ensure that each cell contains only the value (and not the formula). This ensures that the rank order values remain the same if you reorder your data.

Making Sense of Pupil Performance Figures

Monitoring pupils' achievements for classes or cohorts requires periodic summaries of relevant assessments and, possibly, comparisons with other assessments at other points in time. This section illustrates ways in which performance figures can be presented without loss of information and shows how to do this as fairly as possible.

The way in which information is lost through certain forms of reporting can be illustrated by considering a report that, at Key Stage 1, 60 per cent of pupils in each of two classes achieved level 2. By summarising the information in this way, no account is taken of the fact that, in one class, none of the pupils reached level 3, in contrast to the other class in which 60 per cent of pupils reached levels 2A or 3.

The information could be presented most accurately by means of a histogram. Producing a histogram for Key Stage pupils involves counting the numbers of pupils at each level before constructing the graph. Both of these tasks are labour intensive unless undertaken with the help of a spreadsheet like Excel (see Part 2A, p. 47; Part 2B, p. 61).

Reload your school file ([File] [Open . .] [Look in] [3½ Floppy (A)] and highlight your file KS197v2.XLS before clicking on 'Open').

CREATING A HISTOGRAM

Before creating a histogram you must decide on the values to be represented by bars. For this example, we have shown this as a small table (see Screen 9, cells I1:J7). The information (codes) in column J is essential for the histogram. Column I in the table is included for reference and also to enable us to 'improve' the histogram later by the automatic insertion of correct labels. (*Note*: Excel uses the generic term 'Chart' for all its graphical outputs.)

Your first step is to select [Tools] [Data Analysis] [Histogram] before clicking on OK. This leads to the screen with the histogram dialog box presented as Screen 9.

Note: If 'Data Analysis' is not present in the 'Tools' column it will have to be installed. This procedure is described in the Help menu under 'Add-ins'.

Screen 9 shows the options selected for the production of the maths data histogram and some of the information which is needed.

	G	H	I	J	K	L	M	N	O	P	Q
1	MathsT/T	ScSubLvl	level	Code							
2	2.25	2	W	1.5							
3	2.25	2	1	2							
4	2	1	2C	2.25							
5	2.25	2	2B	2.5							
6	2.75	3	2A	2.75							
7	2.5	2	3	3							
8	2.75	3									
9	2.25	2									
10	2.25	1									
11	2.5	2									
12	2.25	2									
13	2.5	2									
14	2.5	2									
15	2	2									
16	2.25	2									

Histogram dialogue box (overlaid):

Input
Input Range: $G$1:$G$69
Bin Range: $J$1:$J$7
☑ Labels

Output options
⦿ Output Range: $I$9
○ New Worksheet Ply:
○ New Workbook
☐ Pareto (sorted histogram)
☐ Cumulative Percentage
☑ Chart Output

OK   Cancel   Help

Sheet4 \ Sheet1 / Sheet2 / Sheet3 /

Screen 9

By highlighting the entire column including the heading MathsT/T (Maths Test/ Task performance figures) this is entered as the 'Input Range'. The cursor must then be moved to the 'Bin Range', and the cells J1 to J7 highlighted. 'Labels' and 'Output Range' are then checked (clicked) and the cell I9 selected as the cell to be the top left corner of the output range. The 'Chart Output' box should also be checked.

Note: the Bin Range consists of the values to be represented by each column in the histogram. Thus the columns will show the frequency of occurrence of scores of 1.5 or less; greater than 1.5 but no more than 2; greater than 2 but no more than 2.25 etc. (Continuous scales are dealt with similarly.)

If the dialogue box is in an inconvenient place on your screen, you can change its position by moving the pointer to anywhere on the blue bar at the top of the box, before holding down the left mouse key, and dragging the box to a new location.

When 'OK' is checked, the output shown in Screen 10 is obtained.

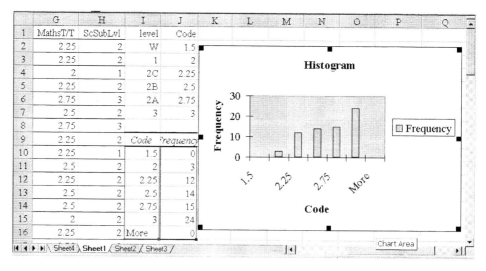

	G	H	I	J	K	L	M	N	O	P	Q
1	MathsT/T	ScSubLvl	level	Code							
2	2.25	2	W	1.5							
3	2.25	2	1	2							
4	2	1	2C	2.25							
5	2.25	2	2B	2.5							
6	2.75	3	2A	2.75							
7	2.5	2	3	3							
8	2.75	3									
9	2.25	2	Code	Frequency							
10	2.25	1	1.5	0							
11	2.5	2	2	3							
12	2.25	2	2.25	12							
13	2.5	2	2.5	14							
14	2.5	2	2.75	15							
15	2	2	3	24							
16	2.25	2	More	0							

Sheet4 \ Sheet1 / Sheet2 / Sheet3 /

Screen 10

Your output screen may differ in some respects from that shown in Screen 10 because the chart has been moved and enlarged to make it clear. You can modify your chart by clicking on a blank part of the chart area and, while holding the left key down, dragging the chart to where you want it. You can alter the size by clicking on a handle (one of the eight black squares) and, when the cursor changes to a double headed arrow, dragging the handle until the histogram is the size you require.

The histogram that is provided by default (automatically) is rather crude and should be improved. You may find it useful when making comparisons to show frequencies as percentages rather than as numbers. The next few pages explain how to achieve this and how to improve the appearance of your histogram.

An Improved Histogram

Before constructing and refining the histogram, percentages can be calculated from the frequency table in the way shown in Screen 11. *Note:* we have not retained the rank orders previously inserted in column I. This was deleted by highlighting column I (click on the column letter 'I') and then pressing the delete key.

	G	H	I	J	K	L	M	N	O	P	
1	MathsT/T	ScSubLvl	level	Code							
2	2.25	2	W	1.5							
3	2.25	2	1	2							
4	2	1	2C	2.25							
5	2.25	2	2B	2.5							
6	2.75	3	2A	2.75							
7	2.5	2	3	3							
8	2.75	3									
9	2.25	2	Code	Frequency							
10	2.25	1	1.5	0	0.0%	=J10/K16					
11	2.5	2	2	3	4.4%	=J11/K16					
12	2.25	2	2.25	12	17.6%	=J12/K16					
13	2.5	2	2.5	14	20.6%	=J13/K16					
14	2.5	2	2.75	15	22.1%	=J14/K16					
15	2	2	3	24	35.3%	=J15/K16					
16	2.25	2	More	0	68	=SUM(J10:J15)					

Sheet4 \ Sheet1 / Sheet2 / Sheet3 /

Screen 11

First, you enter the formulae used to calculate the total number of pupils and the percentages at each level. These are shown in a separate text box beside the relevant cells. Each frequency value is divided by the total (68) in cell K16 and shown as a percentage because the relevant cells have been formatted as percentages – highlight cells K10:K15 and click on [Format] [Cells] [Number].

Note: The formulae can be entered most efficiently by writing =J10/K$16 in cell K10 and then copying and pasting it into the other five cells. The $ placed before the 16 makes this an absolute row reference which does not change as the formula is pasted into the other cells.

To construct the improved histogram, highlight the cells that contain the figures to be used for its construction (K10:K15).

Now use the mouse to click on the 'Chart Wizard' shown here.
The menu as shown in Screen 12 appears.

This enables you to choose the type of chart you require. In this case it is the 'Column' histogram, which has been highlighted automatically (by default). The first, and simplest, chart sub-type has also been highlighted.

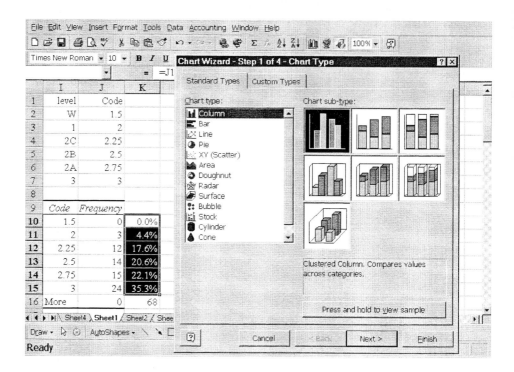

Screen 12

Click on 'Finish' to generate your chart. Click and hold on to one of the corner handles and drag it until the chart fills the screen. With the chart at a good size it is easy to refine the presentation.

Your chart should look like that shown in Chart 1.

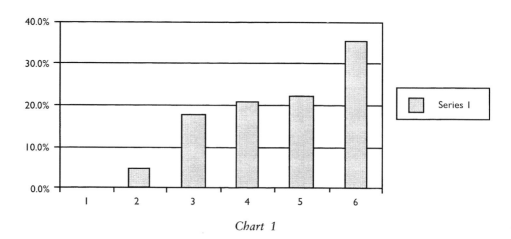

Chart 1

Now, to make the chart presentable, click inside but close to the frame and complete the following operations.

To change fonts
[Format] [Selected chart area] [Font] and select the font and size required. A font size of about 8 points is probably appropriate. Font sizes for specific locations can be selected subsequently.

Adding titles and labels
Click on [Chart] [Chart options] [Titles].
  Enter an appropriate title in the 'Chart title' box (e.g. Mathematics Key Stage 1 percentages at each level) and a label (Level) in the 'Category (X) axis'.
  Select [Legend] and uncheck (click) 'Show legend' to remove the legend (in our example it includes the word 'Series1') which, for this chart, is not needed.
  To display the values above each bar, select [Data labels] and check 'Show value'. Then click on OK.
  To provide the correct labels for each bar select [Chart] [Source data] [Series] and click on 'Category (X) axis labels:' and highlight cells I2:I7 (where the labels are located) before clicking OK.

Changing the appearance of the chart background and bars
To change the plot area background, double click on the plot area and, to remove any colour, check the box 'None' in the section headed 'Area' and click OK.
  To change the colour and pattern of the bars, double click on one of the bars and then select the colour required. To select a pattern use – [Fill effects] [Pattern] select the pattern and background required and then OK. (The effectiveness of the pattern selected will depend upon the characteristics of the printer in use.)
  Before leaving the 'Format data Series . . .' menu, if you wish to change the width of the bars select [Options] and modify the width of the bars to suit before clicking OK.
  Having clicked on the Y axis, select [Format] [Selected axis . . .] [Number] and set the number of decimal places required. (Alternatively double click on the axis to obtain the menu.)
  The resulting histogram is reproduced in Chart 2.

COMPARING TWO OR MORE SETS OF DATA

The histogram provides one of the most informative ways of comparing two sets of information. We shall illustrate how a histogram can be used to compare the performance of boys and girls in Mathematics Key Stage 1. You may wish to copy your data and paste them to another sheet. You can select another sheet by clicking on 'sheet2' or 'sheet3' alongside the bottom scroll bar and then pasting in your data.
  Highlight all your data (you must be particularly careful to include it all) and use [Data] [Sort] and Sort by 'SEX' or 'Column A' and OK to reorder the data. You can use the procedures, already described, to construct separate frequency tables for boys and girls to calculate percentages. Arrange the percentages in adjacent

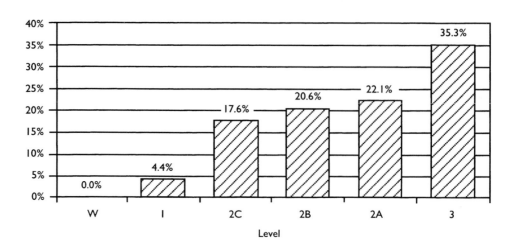

Chart 2 Mathematics Key Stage 1 percentages at each level

columns, as shown below, so that you can use them with the 'Chart Wizard' to construct the histogram. (Remember, if your figures are in the wrong place, you can move them to a convenient location by 'cutting and pasting' – either by means of the Edit menu or with the 'Ctrl & X' keys to 'cut' and the 'Ctrl & V' keys to paste.)

To construct the histogram, highlight the two columns containing the percentages (include the headings 'Boys' and 'Girls') and then click on the 'Chart Wizard'. Having selected 'column' at step 1, click on 'Next>' and, if the resulting screen is correct, click on the word 'Series' at the top of the screen. Now click in the box adjacent to the words 'Category (X) axis labels:' before highlighting column I1:I7.

Level	Boys	Girls
W	0.0%	0.0%
1	5.9%	2.9%
2C	20.6%	14.7%
2B	17.6%	23.5%
2A	20.6%	23.5%
3	35.3%	35.3%

If subsequent steps appear to be as you wish, click on 'Next>' until you reach step 4 when you will probably want to select 'As object in sheet 1:' before clicking on 'Finish'.

Chart 3 illustrates what you can achieve.

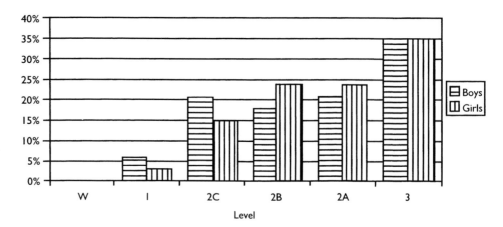

Chart 3 Mathematics Key Stage 1 – performance by gender

Note: you can modify your finished histogram by selecting it (click on it) and then using the Chart Wizard to modify any of the steps you wish to change.

With only a little practice, with the data for English and science, and comparisons for FSM (pupils taking free school meals) and other variables, you will find that you can speed up the process.

Issues for Consideration

At one of two schools in the LEA, 83 per cent of pupils achieved level 2 or better in Key Stage 1 Writing Test/Task. The corresponding figure for pupils at another school is 91 per cent. A histogram showing the distribution of scores for each of these schools is reproduced in Chart 4.

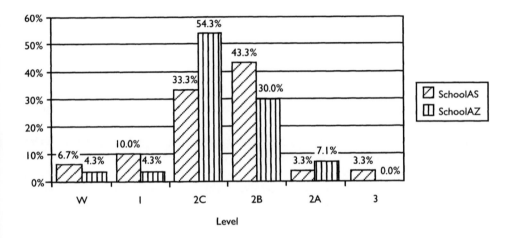

Chart 4 Writing Test/Task results for two schools

The published performance figures for these two schools suggest that the performance of SchoolAZ's pupils (91 per cent) is considerably better than that of SchoolAS pupils (83 per cent). An examination of the results by means of the histogram, however, raises questions about such a conclusion.

Although SchoolAZ has a greater proportion of pupils achieving level 2 or better, these pupils were less successful in achieving levels above 2C. A greater percentage of SchoolAS pupils were, however, in the category 'Working towards'. If each pupil is assigned a numeric value (1.5, 2, 2.25, 2.5, 2.75 and 3 for each level) then the overall average scores achieved by each school is 2.3.

Which school is judged to have achieved the best results is clearly a function of the weights attached to each level of performance and a final decision depends upon the relative importance attributed to the highest and lowest grades achieved.

This example illustrates just one of the issues that can be highlighted by the use of a histogram and should be addressed before making judgements about the performance of groups of pupils.

How Can We Describe Performance?

Although the histogram is one of the best ways of conveying comprehensive information about pupil performance, there are circumstances in which alternatives are preferable. Suppose, for example, that you wished to compare the performance of your pupils with that of those in your local authority, or in England and Wales. One way is to know the marks exceeded by (say) 10 or 20 or 30 per cent of all pupils. You could also aggregate your own figures over several years and compare successive results with the accumulated data. The following example shows how Excel can be used to find, very quickly, the marks exceeded by 10 or 20 per cent or any other percentage of your pupils. It automatically provides each pupil with a rank order.

CALCULATING PERCENTILES; QUARTILES, MEDIAN, MODE

Examples of percentiles are the tenth percentile (P_{10}), the mark below which 10 per cent of pupils' marks lie and the ninetieth percentile (P_{90}), the mark below which 90 per cent of marks lie. We shall use the data to calculate the percentiles and rank orders of the pupils in the Writing Test/Task. To do this, first copy (Ctrl & C) the first seven columns (A to G) of your data and paste them (Ctrl & V) to a new worksheet. (If necessary you can create additional sheets by means of [Insert] [Worksheet].)

You will find it helpful to insert a new column to the left of the one with pupil names and then to number each pupil sequentially. (We describe a quick way of doing this on p. 14.)

If you still have your data in the order of surnames, and with the boys first, the first part of your data should now look like Table 3.

Now, from the menu bar, select [Tools] [Data Analysis . . .] [Rank and Percentile] OK and then highlight the cells G1:G69 and this range will be inserted automatically in the Rank and Percentile box. Next, click on the 'Labels in First

Table 3

	Surname	First name	Sex	Nurs	FSM	Write T/T	Maths T/T
1	Adams	John	1	1	1	2.25	2.25
2	Andrews	Geoffrey	1	1	2	2.5	2.75
3	Bennet	Peter	1	1	2	3	3
4	Bowen	Peter	1	1	2	3	3
5	Brain	Richard	1	1	2	2.25	2.75
6	Brown	John	1	1	2	2.25	2.5
7	Burton	Reg	1	2	2	3	3
8	Burton	Alistair	1	1	2	2.5	3
9	Cane	Sean	1	1	2	2.25	2.75

Row' box to indicate that the heading WriteT/T has been included. Finally, click on the circle to the left of 'Output range:'. Click on the box next to it and enter $K$1 (or the cell which is to be the top left hand corner of your output).

Your screen should look like the one reproduced as Screen 13.

Screen 13

Click on OK to obtain the table, part of which is shown in Table 4.

The first column, headed 'Point', contains the row number of the pupil with a 'WriteT/T' score of 3. He is one of nine pupils with the highest mark (i.e. Rank 1) and the figure '88.00%' in the 'Percent' column shows their percentile (they have achieved higher scores than 88 per cent of pupils).

In this case, the full table provides information about the performance of a small number of pupils with few mark alternatives. A description of how to calculate percentile points is provided in Part 2A (pp. 49–50).

You may want to identify pupils by names rather than by numbers. This deficiency can easily be done by one of two methods.

Table 4

Point	Write T/T	Rank	Percent
3	3	1	88.00%
4	3	1	88.00%
7	3	1	88.00%
15	3	1	88.00%
28	3	1	88.00%
35	3	1	88.00%
60	3	1	88.00%
61	3	1	88.00%
63	3	1	88.00%
14	2.75	10	74.60%
31	2.75	10	74.60%
34	2.75	10	74.60%
38	2.75	10	74.60%
46	2.75	10	74.60%

The simplest form of attaching names to the pupil numbers is to sort the table in the order of the pupil numbers and then to copy and paste the names alongside.

An alternative method which can be useful in other circumstances is to use our list of names, with their row numbers, as a 'vertical lookup table', and use the numbers in our new table to ensure that a copy of each name is located where we want it.

Percentile points at 10 per cent intervals are usually sufficient to describe a distribution of marks and these particular points are sometimes referred to as deciles with D_1 corresponding to P_{10}, D_2 to P_{20} etc.

How You Can Create and Use a Vertical Lookup Table

You can use the list of numbers and names in cells A2:B69 as your lookup table. There is no reason to restrict the table to just two columns if you wish to use first names, or information contained in other rows.

The Excel formula, in cell J2, needed to obtain the first correct name (Bennet, No. 3 in our list) is shown in Diagram 1.

You can now copy cell J2 (Ctrl & C) and paste it (Ctrl & V) into the rest of column J. (Note that, as you paste the cell down the column, the row number of the 'lookup cell' changes but the $ signs ensure that there is no corresponding change to the location of the lookup table.)

When you copy part of the resulting table, it is sensible when you paste to the new location to use [Edit] [Paste special] and then click on Values. This ensures that only the names, without formulae, are pasted and reduces the possibility of errors.

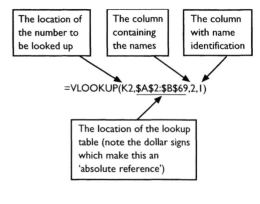

Diagram 1

Finding a Few Percentile Points Quickly and Simply

Here is an alternative, and rapid, way in which you can use Excel to calculate percentiles. It is particularly useful when you wish to obtain only a few points (say P_{50}, the median and P_{25} and P_{75}, the quartiles). First, enter 0.25, 0.5 and 0.75 in a column at any convenient place in your spreadsheet. You can, if you wish, format these values as percentages [Format] [Cells . . .] [Percentage] and select two decimal places so that they appear as 25.00%, 50.00% and 75.00%.

Click on the cell immediately to the right of the cell containing 0.25 and then on [Insert] [Function] [Statistical] [PERCENTILE] and OK. Now click in the box immediately to the right of the word 'Array' and highlight the column of pupil scores for the 'Write Test/Task' marks (G2:G69). (If you wish to move the menu box out of the way just click on a blank part and drag it to a more convenient place.) Now click in the box beside the letter 'k' and then click on the cell in the spreadsheet containing the value 0.25 (or 25 per cent) and then click on OK.

Your formula will have provided the answer 2.25 which is P_{25}, the mark below which 25 per cent of marks lie. With the distribution of marks in our example this value is the best possible. (You should be aware that the procedure used by Excel to calculate percentiles is less complex than that used in the more precise method described in Part 2A, pp. 44–5 which is appropriate when using larger numbers.)

The formula used to calculate the percentile is '=PERCENTILE(G2:G69,J6)'. To create corresponding formulae alongside the other percentiles you could copy and paste this cell. First, however, you *must* insert $ signs before the row numbers to change the formula to '=PERCENTILE(G$2:G$69,J6)' so that as you paste it down it continues to work with the same array (G2:G69). (The dollar sign ensures that the row numbers remain unchanged.)

Quartiles

The three values which divide a score distribution into four sectors are often used as descriptors and are termed 'Quartile points'. P_{25} is the first quartile point (Q_1), P_{50} is the second quartile point (Q_2) and P_{75} is the third quartile point (Q_3). These can be obtained directly in a similar way to the percentile points. Q_1 is obtained by inserting the function 'QUARTILE', entering 1 against 'Quart' and clicking OK. In the box labelled Quart insert 1, 2 or 3 to obtain Q_1, Q_2 or Q_3; 0 and 4 return the minimum and maximum values respectively.

The Median

The second quartile point (Q_2) is the 'middlemost' point that divides the score scale so that half of the scores lie above it and half lie below it. This point is called the middlemost and is termed the 'median'. Unlike the mean, the median has the advantage that a few extremely high, or extremely low, scores do not influence it. So there are occasions when it is the preferred way to describe 'central tendency'. Excel can provide the median value by means of [Insert] [Function] [Statistical] [MEDIAN].

The Mode

The mode in a set of scores is a value that occurs most frequently when compared with those in its immediate vicinity. It is thus possible to have more than one mode in a set of scores. Excel can be used to obtain the mode ([Insert] [Function] [Statistical] [MODE]) but this function is really only of use when you already have some knowledge about the distribution. (For discussion of these measures see Part 2A; pp. 43–6, 54–5.)

COMPARING THE PERFORMANCE OF SEVERAL SCHOOLS

In some areas, groups of schools provide each other with information via the LEA. This information is then used to inform the process of monitoring and target setting. Although we could use the bar chart to compare the performance of pupils at two or three schools, it becomes more difficult to interpret when it is used to show the distribution of scores from several schools. The 'hilo' chart, illustrated by Chart 5, 'Reception class reading performance', provides an alternative to the histogram and, by reducing the amount of information provided, allows simple comparisons to be made with many more schools.

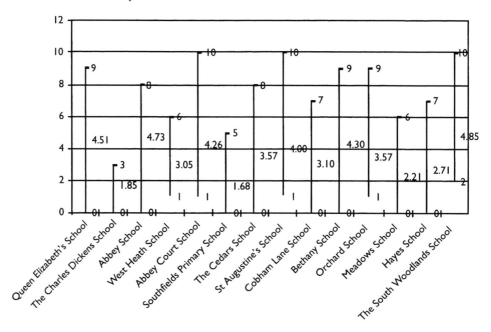

Chart 5 Reception class reading performance

LEA data in the form of one column with school names and three columns in the order 'minimum', 'mean' and 'maximum' was used to create Chart 5 by means of a procedure similar to that used for the histogram, but selecting 'stock' as the 'Chart type:' followed by the appropriate 'Chart sub-type option:'. Appendix 3 includes the mean scores from these and other schools.

Although the hilo chart shows the minimum, mean and maximum scores for each school, it does not indicate whether the bulk of scores are spread throughout the range of scores or clustered about the mean, which would be a preferable distribution.

We can overcome this disadvantage by creating a table that incorporates a measure of 'spread'. In the example the table from which the chart was constructed includes the four data columns 'mean + standard deviation', 'highest score', 'lowest score' and 'mean – standard deviation'. (See standard deviation (SD) in Part 2A, pp. 45–6.)

Chart 6 uses an Excel feature which, although designed primarily for business applications, serves our need for a simple means of comparing the performance of schools without sacrificing some relevant information. It was obtained by selecting 'stock' as the 'Chart type:' followed by the second 'Chart sub-type option:'.

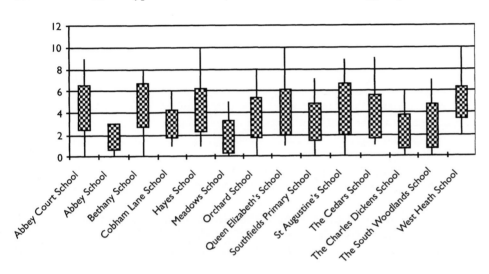

Chart 6 Reception class reading performance (showing spread)

Note: in order to include school names, when at step 2 select 'Series' click on the Category (X) axis labels box and then highlight the column of school names.

HOW CAN WE COMBINE MARKS?

Key Stage results published by the Department for Education and Employment (DfEE) are presented for each subject. The media, however, invariably use an averaged score to rank schools and LEAs. There is a long history in education of adding scores for different subjects to provide overall performance figures, but this can introduce one form of error shown by this extreme illustration using examination marks.

	English	Maths.	Science	Mean
Andrew	89	48	48	61.7
Brian	52	51	49	50.7
Colin	21	52	53	42.0

The marks for English, mathematics and science have been averaged and show that Andrew achieved the best overall marks, followed by Brian with Colin coming last. If we look at these results in a different way, we see that Andrew came first in

English, but came last in both mathematics and science. Colin came first in both mathematics and science, and came last only in English and could reasonably have expected to be placed first overall. The reason for this apparent contradiction is that the 'spread' of marks in English was so great that results in the other two examinations cannot outweigh the effect of doing well, or badly, in English.

This example, although oversimplistic, illustrates one of the ways in which the spread of marks can be important. There are many other occasions when it is essential to be able to measure the spread, as well as the mean value, of marks.

THE SPREAD OF MARKS; AVERAGE DEVIATION, VARIANCE, STANDARD DEVIATION

A simple way of measuring the spread of marks is to subtract the mean mark from each pupil's mark. Each pupil would then be assigned a new mark, positive for marks higher than the mean and negative if lower. In this way we could indicate the extent to which each pupil's mark exceeded, or fell short of, the average. By calculating the mean of the absolute values of this new set of marks we would have a measure of the average spread (termed 'average deviation'). The term 'absolute' indicates that the negative signs are all ignored (otherwise the result would always be zero). In Excel this can be achieved by enclosing formulae in ABS() so that, for example, =G2-G$70 would become =ABS(G2-G$70). In this example the cell G70 contains the mean of all the scores and the dollar sign has been inserted so that, when copied down the column, the cell reference does not change.

Average Deviation

When we require only the average deviation this can be obtained immediately by using [Insert] [Function] [Statistical] [AVEDEV] and highlighting the relevant array of marks (see Part 2A, p. 45).

Variance

Variance is a more widely used measure of the 'spread' of marks and can be obtained by [Insert] [Function] [Statistical] [VARP]. (This and the function 'VAR' which is used to estimate the population variance from a sample is dealt with in greater detail on p. 46.)

Variance is obtained by first subtracting the mean mark from each pupil's mark and squaring the resulting figure. The variance is the mean of all these squared figures. 'Standard deviation', which is the square root of variance, is usually used in preference to variance as the measure of 'spread' (see Part 2A, p. 46).

Standard Deviation (SD)

The standard deviation can be calculated directly by [Insert] [Function] [Statistical] [STDEVP]. In practice it attaches greater weight to outlying scores than would be the case with the mean deviation. (If you are using a sample to estimate the standard deviation of a population, then you should use the function STDEV.)

Standardised Scores

You can convert different sets of marks so that every set has the same mean and standard deviation so that every pupil's marks in different subjects, or parts of an assessment, could be added without giving undue weight to that with the greatest spread of marks. One way of achieving this is to subtract the mean score from every pupil's mark and then to divide each resulting figure by the standard deviation. These are usually referred to as z scores (see Part 2A, pp. 50–1).

Screen 14 shows how the set of MathsT/T scores could be converted into z scores. The mean MathsT/T score is located in cell G70 and this value has been subtracted from each score in column G to provide 'deviation scores' in column J. The standard deviation of these new scores is located in cell J70 [=STDEVP(J2:J69)] and the first z score calculated in cell K2 [=J2/J$70].

G	H	I	J	K
			=G2-G$70	
WriteT/T	MathsT/T		WriteT/Tdev	z score
2.25	2.25		-0.23	-0.84
2.5	2.75		0.02	0.07
3	3		0.52	1.88
3	3		0.52	1.88
2.25	2.75		-0.23	-0.84

(Note that the $ sign has been inserted before the figure 70 so that when this cell is copied and pasted into the other cells in the column the absolute reference to row 70 remains unchanged.)

Screen 14

Now use Excel to obtain the mean and standard deviation of your new set of z scores. The mean is zero and the standard deviation is '1', as is always the case with z scores. In practice, neither pupils nor parents would be impressed with such low marks, half of which were negative, so it is common practice to multiply each z score by 10 and to add a fixed figure to each mark. Thus you could multiply each of your newly created z scores by 10 and add 50 to provide a more acceptable final mark. (If you create these in column L, cell L2 should contain the formula [=K2*10+50] which you could copy down to obtain all the other pupil marks.) If you have done this correctly your new set of marks should have a mean of 50 and a standard deviation of 10.

How Can We Investigate the Relationships between Sets of Marks?

When you calculated the z scores for the English Test/Task results, you first subtracted the mean from each mark and then divided the resulting figure by the standard deviation. Your new set of marks therefore have a mean of zero and a standard deviation (SD) of 1.

If you repeated this for the MathsTest/Task marks, and added an extra column consisting of the product of each pair of z scores (see Part 2A, pp. 45–6), you would obtain a set of results, the first few rows of which should appear as shown in Table 5.

Table 5

Maths z score	Write z score	Product
−1.34	−0.84	1.12
0.27	0.07	0.02
1.08	1.88	2.02
1.08	1.88	2.02
0.27	−0.84	−0.23
−0.53	−0.84	0.45
1.08	1.88	2.02
1.08	0.07	0.07
0.27	−0.84	−0.23
1.08	0.07	0.07
−1.34	−0.84	1.12
−1.34	−1.75	2.33

If you now calculate the mean of the column headed 'Product', you obtain the value 0.68. This is termed the Pearson product moment correlation coefficient and indicates the extent of agreement between both variables. In this example, it is the correlation between the English and mathematics Test/Tasks (see Part 2B, pp. 76–7).

If the mathematics marks had all been the same as the English marks, the mean of the 'Product' would have been 1. (*Note*: you would have, in effect, just recalculated the standard deviation of the English z scores which is 1.) If the marks had been the same, but with opposite signs, all the resulting products would have been negative and their mean value would be −1. Such a result is extremely unlikely and where the relationship is less than perfect values lie between −1 and +1. If the variables are entirely unrelated, the correlation coefficient would be zero.

We can gain an understanding of the relationship between two variables by plotting one against the other in the form of a scatter diagram. Excel has been used to produce Diagram 2 to provide a visual indication of the relationship between English and mathematics Test/Task scores.

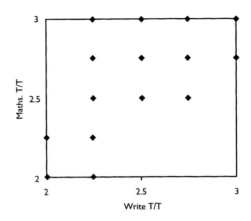

Diagram 2 The relationship between maths and English Test/Tasks

The scatter diagram shows a quite clear tendency for pupils with high scores in the English Test/Task to perform well in the Mathematics Test/Task and vice versa. With only five levels of performance and no indication of the frequency of identical marks in each subject, the plot does not provide full information about individual pupils (see Part 2B; p. 77).

To illustrate how differences between schools may influence target setting, two scatter diagrams have been constructed with variables provided in Appendix 3. Mean values were calculated for information recorded for reception pupils in 61 schools in a single LEA. The first scatter diagram, which shows a strong relationship between performance in reading and mathematics, is shown in Diagram 3 (r=0.803).

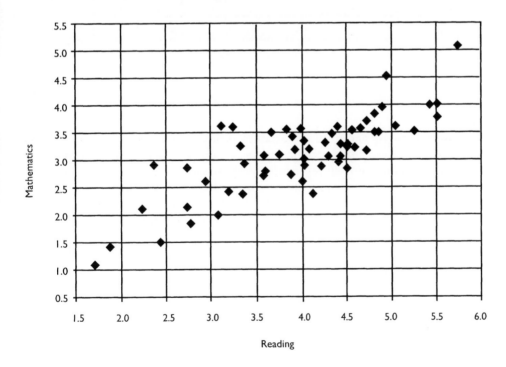

Diagram 3 Mean school reception class performance

It is self-evident that schools in which reception pupils performed well in English also achieved correspondingly good results in mathematics. The correlation between performance in reading and mathematics is represented by the high value of 'r' which is +0.803. Great care must be taken before inferences are drawn about possible reasons for this relationship and the next scatter diagram shows one external factor, 'overcrowding', that might contribute to pupil performance.

Diagram 4 shows the relationship between 'overcrowding' and reading performance. The proportion of households with one or more persons per room in the enumeration district of each pupil's home was assigned to each pupil record. Such information would be of no use in considering the circumstances of individual pupils. The scatter diagram does, however, indicate that there is a general relationship between the reading performance of school reception classes and the level of overcrowding in the immediate areas in which pupils live.

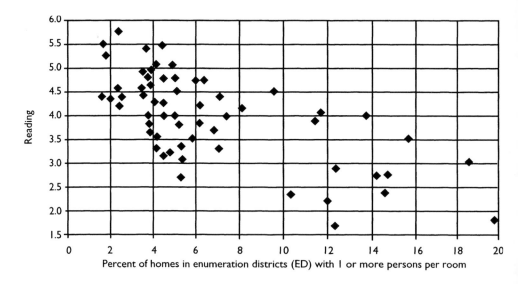

Diagram 4 Reception classes – overcrowding and reading

Consideration of background variables is useful when teachers think about strategies for investigating circumstances which may affect their own pupils' attainments, and monitoring subsequent performance levels.

Diagram 4 clearly indicates the extent to which the reading performance of pupils in schools with pupils recruited from areas with the greatest levels of overcrowding tend to be those with the lowest mean performance figures and vice versa. The correlation between overcrowding and reading performance is –0.670. The negative sign indicates that, in general, schools with high proportions of pupils who live in areas with 'overcrowded' accommodation perform less well than those with lower proportions. Such evidence has implications when considering the relative performance of schools and of educational 'value added' (see Part 2B, pp. 75–9).

The Pearson correlation coefficient provides the most commonly used measure of relationships and is easily calculated with Excel.

THE PEARSON PRODUCT MOMENT CORRELATION COEFFICIENT, INTERPRETATION AND PREDICTION

You will often see the Pearson product moment correlation denoted by the lower case letter 'r' and its full name abbreviated to 'correlation' or to 'correlation coefficient'.

A single correlation coefficient between two variables is obtained in Excel by means of the formula =CORREL(C3:C63,D3:D63) where C3:C63, D3:D63 refer to the two columns of figures to be correlated. This could also be achieved by [Insert] [Function] [Statistical] [CORREL] and then entering (by highlighting if preferred) the references to the two columns of figures in the boxes labelled 'Array 1' and 'Array 2'.

When you wish to obtain all the correlations between several columns of figures, this can be achieved most efficiently by [Tools] [Data Analysis . . .] [Correlation]. In the dialogue box enter the range of data to be correlated and, if you have included variable names, check (click) the 'Labels in first row' box. In the 'Output range:' box enter the reference of the cells into which the correlations are to be pasted. This must consist of one row and one column for each variable. Thus, for example, the correlation matrix shown in Table 6 required that a nine-by-nine output range was entered (this is most readily achieved by highlighting the area required).

Table 6 Correlation matrix generated by Excel for nine variables

	Reading	Writing	Speaking	Maths	FSM	Soc. Class	Qual.	Unempl.	Overcrowd
Reading	1								
Writing	0.739	1							
Speaking	0.539	0.554	1						
Maths.	0.803	0.697	0.540	1					
FSM	−0.244	−0.419	−0.172	−0.260	1				
Soc. Class	0.538	0.434	0.365	0.528	−0.275	1			
Qual.	0.474	0.383	0.340	0.456	−0.345	0.926	1		
Unempl.	−0.506	−0.445	−0.228	−0.501	0.490	−0.661	−0.559	1	
Overcrowd	−0.670	−0.479	−0.307	−0.665	0.049	−0.741	−0.605	0.705	1

The correlation between any two variables can be read from coefficients (values) in the matrix. Thus between reading and writing it is 0.739, and between overcrowding in pupils' home enumeration districts (EDs) and mathematics it is −0.665. Although Excel provides coefficients to more decimal places, they should be reported to three decimal places only (see Part 2B, pp. 81–2).

Correlation and Problems of Interpretation and Prediction

You can gain further insight about the association between reading achievement and overcrowding by drawing a straight line that fits as closely as possible to the points we have entered. Excel inserts the trend line (that is the line that 'best fits' your data) if you click anywhere on your chart and then select [Chart] [Add Trend line . . .] [Linear] and OK. (Excel gets the 'best fit' line by ensuring that the sum of the squares of all the vertical distances between every point and your trend line is the smallest possible.)

Diagram 5 shows the trend line added to your chart. Two additional items of information have been included when adding the trend line by using [Options] and

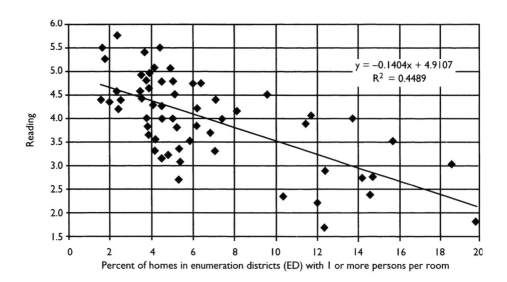

Diagram 5 Reception classes – overcrowding and reading

then checking the boxes 'Display equation on chart' and 'Display R-squared value on chart' before clicking on OK.

In similar circumstances, suppose you wish to estimate the mean English level that you would expect your school to achieve if the mean proportion of overcrowding in the pupils' homes was 4 per cent. You would replace 'X' in the equation $Y = -0.1404X + 4.9107$ with the value 4 and calculate Y (the average reading score) to be 4.349.

You could insert the overcrowding figure in the equation for other schools to obtain their expected average reading scores (these correspond to points on the 'regression line').

We can use Diagram 5 to illustrate a form of question that, with different sets of data, is frequently asked. For these data it would be 'How well does the knowledge of the extent of overcrowding among a school's pupils, enable me to evaluate the school's performance in the reading test?'

For example, pupils at Bradfields School come from areas in which 15.74 per cent of residents live with one or more persons per room. We could read this from our chart or, alternatively, use 15.74 in place of 'X' in our equation 'Y = –0.1404X + 4.9107' to obtain the school's expected average reading test score. Our equation then becomes:

$$Y = -0.1404 \times 15.74 + 4.9107 \text{ which gives } -2.209896 + 4.9107$$

This equals 2.70 (to two decimal places). Therefore, if overcrowding alone decided the school's average reading score, we would expect Bradfields School to have achieved an average of 2.70. In fact Bradfields School achieved a score of 3.54, which is considerably better than expected. It is possible that variables which we could not take into account led to a better performance than we would expect if overcrowding had been the only influence. These variables would include the quality of teaching, the resources of the school, the interest of parents, the abilities of pupils, inadequacies in our data and many other unpredictable influences.

The next question to answer is 'What sort of importance might reasonably be attached to the difference (0.84) between the expected score of 2.70 and the actual achievement of 3.54?' One way of doing this is to place the schools in order of the differences between expected and actual scores. When we do this, we find that Bradfields School moves from forty-fifth to sixth out of 61 schools – a dramatic change.

You could gain a less precise measure by looking at Diagram 5. Measure by eye how far the dot for each school lies above or below the trend line and compare this distance with its overall height. It is important to remember that the changes we have made do not involve changes to the levels achieved by pupils. Our average reading scores still provide the only measure for level of pupil reading performance at each school. Our new way of looking at the data enables us to recognise the extent to which performance is not the sole product of the quality of teaching and to make some allowance for one contextual variable.

Our analyses show clearly that, for whatever reason, the relatively poor performance of some schools is associated with a characteristic of the neighbourhoods in which their pupils live. We have not shown that overcrowding causes poor school performance or that some schools are better than others at overcoming any such disadvantage. We have, however, demonstrated the existence of one important relationship, which should be taken into account if performance figures are to be used to draw inferences about the quality of teaching in these schools.

By squaring the correlation coefficient $(-0.670) \times (-0.670) = 0.4489$ we can calculate how much of the variance in reading scores could be estimated from a knowledge of the overcrowding percentages. In this example almost 44 per cent of the variance can be estimated or, alternatively, about 56 per cent (termed the error variance) cannot be estimated. This leads to a useful means of gauging the importance of a correlation. We can see that a correlation coefficient of 0.2 when squared becomes 0.04 and could therefore be used with only one variable to predict 4 per cent of the variance of the other. To predict 50 per cent of the variance we must have a correlation coefficient which is greater than 0.7. Whether we consider that a correlation coefficient is important or not will depend, in part, on its magnitude and also upon judgements based on the particular circumstances.

Even when there is no relationship between two variables in the population, there is always a chance that we would find a correlation in our sample. The question 'What is the probability of finding a correlation as great as mine if there is no real correlation in the whole population?' needs to be answered before we can decide whether we have found evidence of a real relationship. Fortunately, this question is easily answered with the help of published tables. With a sample of 60, the probability is less than 1 per cent that we would find a correlation with a value as great as ±0.670, the one in our example, if none exists in the population. By convention, if the probability is 5 per cent or less, we would be justified in reporting it as 'significant'.

Confidence in Sample Estimates

THE POPULATION MEAN

If you were to test repeated random samples of (say) 7-year-old pupils and measure their height, you would expect to find differences between the mean (average) height found for each sample. With samples, each of 10,000 pupils, these differences would be very small and you would expect them to be close to the mean height of all 7 year olds in the population. Taking small samples, the differences would be greater and a proportion of them would be quite different from the population mean (see Part 2B, pp. 62–4).

Excel enables you to convert your mean score into a range of values which you could be 95 per cent confident would span the mean of the population. (This means that out of 100 repeated samples like yours, 95 would span the population mean.) With reasonably large samples, you can calculate this confidence interval by subtracting 1.96×'standard error' from your sample mean to find the lower boundary and adding it to your sample mean to obtain the higher boundary. With our sample of only 68 pupils, we should use the larger value of 2.00 in place of the 1.96 to calculate the standard error. A description of how you obtain this value is provided in Part 2B (p. 64).

You can use Excel to calculate the standard error by dividing the standard deviation of the population by the square root of the number in your sample. Unfortunately, you probably do not know the standard deviation of the population so you must estimate it from your sample. Excel does this for you when you use the formula 'STDEV'. This provides a slightly greater value than would be obtained with 'STDEVP', which assumes that your data are the entire population.

You can calculate the standard error in one step by typing the following:

STDEV(F2:F69)*2/SQRT(68)

This multiplies the 'estimate of the standard deviation of the population' using data in cells F2 to F69 by two before dividing it by the square root of the number in the sample [SQRT(68)]. This gives a value of 0.06737 for the Writing Test/Task scores.

We can thus be 95 per cent confident that 2.481618±0.067337 spans the true mean. Or alternatively, we can be 95 per cent confident that the range 2.414281 to 2.548955 spans the true mean. We have included more decimal places than are sensible and you would probably prefer to express the range as 2.41 to 2.55.

A useful alternative method is to use [Insert] [Tools] [Data Analyses . . .] and then to check the 'Summary statistics' and 'Confidence Level for Mean' boxes. This provides several statistics including a slightly more precise estimate of the confidence interval.

The standard error of the mean (SE_m) is useful when comparing school or class results with information from cohorts, such as the LEA population, standardisation samples to see whether your group would be 'significantly different' had it been a random sample (see Part 2B, p. 61).

DIFFERENCE BETWEEN GROUP MEANS

We quite often observe differences between the performance of groups of children, but are unsure whether this is a 'real' difference or is the result of 'chance'. With the data for 68 pupils used in our examples, the girls achieved better results than the boys and it would be useful to know whether the difference is such that it would be reasonable to assume that it has not come about by 'chance'. If there is really no difference between the performance of boys and girls in the population we would expect that, if we repeatedly used very large samples, most of the differences found would be close to zero. With small samples these differences would be greater (see Part 2A, p. 68).

Using [Insert] [Tools] [Data Analyses . . .] and then checking 't-Test: Two-Sample Assuming Unequal Variances' and 'OK' will obtain Screen 15 in which values have been inserted. The range of cells in which writing Test/Task results for boys are located in 'Variable 1 Range:' and for girls in 'Variable 2 Range:'.

Screen 15

The resulting Excel output is shown in Table 7.

Table 7 t-Test: Two-Sample Assuming Unequal Variances

	Write T/Tb	Write T/Tg
Mean	2.4559	2.5074
Variance	0.0889	0.0662
Observations	34	34
Hypothesised mean difference	0	
df	65	
t Stat	−0.7620	
P(T<=t) one-tail	0.2244	
t Critical one-tail	1.6686	
P(T<=t) two-tail	0.4488	
t Critical two-tail	1.9971	

Using the more conservative 'two-tail' test, the result shows that, with these rather small samples, a 't Stat' value of 0.762 is below the critical value of 1.9971. This means that there is insufficient evidence to reject the null hypothesis that there is no difference in the population.

THE CONTINGENCY TABLE

Table 8 shows the performance of boys and girls, in one local authority, in their Key Stage 2 Writing Test/Task. The table has been constructed in Excel and row and column totals provided to the right and below.

Table 8 Writing Test/Task: observed frequencies (O$_f$)

	W	I	2C	2B	2A	3	
Boys	138	230	477	390	162	35	1,432
Girls	69	135	454	408	227	57	1,350
	207	365	931	798	389	92	2,782

You can see from quite a casual inspection that there are fewer girls than boys in the 'Working towards' category and more girls than boys in the highest category, which indicates that girls appear to be rather more successful than the boys. It would be helpful to gain an indication as to whether this is because girls, in general, are better than boys at the Writing Test/Task, or the result of sampling variation.

You can use Excel to calculate the frequencies to be expected if there were no difference in the performance of boys and girls. Our first task is to calculate the overall proportions of boys and girls. That is 1,432÷2,782 and 1,350÷2,782 respectively. These proportions are shown to the right of Table 9, which shows expected frequencies, and have been used to calculate the 'expected frequencies' for boys and girls. (We would expect 0.515 times the number of pupils in the 'W' category to be boys and 0.485 times this number to be girls, thus 0.515 × 207 = 106.6 and 0.485 × 207 = 100.4.)

If there were no difference in the writing abilities of boys and girls, we would expect the proportions of boys and girls in each category (W, 1, 2C etc.) to be the

Table 9 Writing Test/Task: expected frequencies (E_f)

	W	I	2C	2B	2A	3	
Boys	106.6	187.9	479.2	410.8	200.2	47.4	0.515
Girls	100.4	177.1	451.8	387.2	188.8	44.6	0.485
	207	365	931	798	389	92	

same as the overall proportions. We can therefore calculate the expected frequencies for boys by multiplying the total number of pupils in each category by the overall proportion of boys (e.g. we would expect to find $207 \times 0.515 = 106.6$ boys in the 'W' category). The process is then repeated for girls.

By comparing the expected with the observed frequencies, you can see that the performance of the girls is better, and the performance of the boys is worse, than we would have expected if they were of equal standard.

The important question to answer now is 'What is the probability that the differences between observed and expected frequencies have come about by chance and are not the result of actual differences in the population?' The first step in finding an answer to this question is to calculate the Chi-square value (χ^2). This is obtained by first calculating $(O_f - E_f)^2 \div E_f$ for each cell in our table and then adding all of these values. This has been achieved in Excel and the resulting Chi-square table is Table 10.

Table 10 Chi-square

	W	I	2C	2B	2A	3
Boys	9.283	9.443	0.010	1.049	7.300	3.224
Girls	9.846	10.017	0.011	1.113	7.744	3.420

The sum of the values in each of the cells in Table 10 is 62.460 ($\chi^2 = 62.460$).

The answer to our question 'What is the probability that the differences between observed and expected frequencies have come about by chance and are not the result of real differences?' can be found from a table that shows the distribution of values of χ^2. An account of how to achieve this is included in Part 2B (p. 75). In this example, if there were no actual difference in the Writing Test/Task performance of boys and girls in the population, a value of χ^2 as great as 62 would occur in less than 0.1 per cent of such comparisons. We can then state that our result – that girls perform better than boys in the Writing Test/Task – is significant at the 0.1 per cent level (sometimes expressed as P<0.01).

Creating an Expectancy Table

Although the scatter diagram provides an excellent means of examining the relationships between two sets of data, there are occasions when it is useful to know the number of identical pairs of values. Sometimes you can categorise one or both score ranges into bands and pair pupils by their band groups rather than individual scores (see Part 2B, p. 79). In this example Surrey maintained schools with similar percentages of pupils awarded five or more grades A to C passes at GCSE in 1997 were allocated to groups according to the percentages on the SEN register in each school (1997 published data).

Our method is to use a lookup table (see p. 24) to categorise both sets of scores.

A small portion of the data and lookup table has been reproduced in Table 11. You can see that from the lookup table that GCSE percentages of 16 to below 21 have been allocated the code 1, those from 21 to below 26 were allocated 2, those from 26 to below 31 were allocated 3, and so on. Columns 2 and 3 in the lookup table serve the same purpose for the percentages of SEN pupils as Columns 1 and 3 did for the GCSE results.

Table 11

Surrey data		Lookup table			Re-coded	
GCSE%	SEN%	GCSE%	SEN%	Code	GCSE%	SEN%
46	21	16	0	1	7	7
26	24	21	4	2	3	8
57	13	26	7	3	9	5
49	11	31	10	4	7	4
66	7	36	13	5	11	3
24	22	41	16	6	2	8

The formula used to provide the first value (46) with the code '7' is =VLOOKUP(B3,$H$3:$J$20,3) where 'B' is the column with the GCSE results and $H$3:$J$20 defines the lookup table. (The $ signs indicate that these are 'absolute' references and will therefore not change when the cells are copied down the column.) The figure 3 in the formula refers to the column in the lookup table that contains the codes.

A similar formula [=VLOOKUP(C3,$I$3:$J$13,2)] allocates code 7 to the SEN% value of 21 and has been copied down to provide all the other codes.

The new sets of values provided in this way have been used to construct a table that records our codes for SEN in separate columns for each category of GCSE results. Part of this table is shown in Table 12 and hence '8' appears in the column headed '3' when this refers to a school with code '3' for its GCSE results.

Table 12

Re-coded				GCSE codes				
GCSE%	SEN%			1	2	3	4	5
7	7							
3	8					8		
9	5							
7	4							
11	3							
2	8				8			
5	4							4
3	10					10		
5	2							2

Every cell in our new table contains a copy of the formula =IF($E4=I$3,$F4," ") located in the top left cell in our table. This works as follows: if E4 (the cell with the GCSE code '7') is equal to the value in cell I3, it assumes the value of E4; if it is not equal " " – (blank) is displayed. The $ signs ensure that when the cell is copied to other cells in the table each formula changes appropriately. This formula when copied into the cell containing the first eight in the column headed '3' becomes =IF($E5=K$3,$F5," ") which provides the value 8.

Our final stage is to count and record the occurrences of each SEN code in each column of GCSE results.

To achieve Chart 7, the formula =COUNTIF(I$4:I$68,$F74) was typed into the top left cell and then copied throughout the chart. It counts the occurrences of the

SEN%	16–20	21–25	26–30	31–35	36–40	41–45	46–50	51–55	56–60	61–65	66–70	71–75	76–80	81–85	86–90	91–95	96–100
28–30			1		1												
25–27	1	1								1							
22–24		1	1								1						
19–21				1		1	1		1								
16–18	1							1	1								
13–15					3	3			5	2					1	1	
10–12		1				1	2	1	2	2	1						
7–9							2	2	1		3	1	1				
4–6				1				1	1	2							2
0–3												1	1		1	1	2

Chart 7 Percentages gaining 5 or more GCSEs at level C or higher

value 10 in the column I4:I68. The value '10' is located in cell F74 and you can see that there is one such value (which corresponds to between 28 and 30 per cent SEN) in the cell with GCSE results between 26 and 30 per cent. Values in column F (not shown) correspond to the SEN codes so that F75 has the value 9, F76 has the value 8, and so on.

Column and row labels have been inserted and zeros displayed as blanks by means of [Tools] [Options . . .] [View] and uncheck 'Zero values'.

The chart can be used for comparisons or forecasts. For instance, in Surrey schools with 22 per cent or more pupils on the SEN register could expect to have about 30 per cent awarded five or more good GCSEs. Aggregation of data over, say, three years would firm up these expectancies. Of course, schools successfully meeting targets aimed at reducing numbers on the register would contribute to changing expectations. Also, schools would vary their forecast targets according to variations in the proportion of pupils registered as having special needs in a particular year. Guidance for individual pupils could be achieved in much the same way by creating lookup tables for an attainment measure or ability test given in, say, Year 9 and accumulating expectancy data (see Part 2B, p. 79).

Part 2A
Scales and their Interpretation

This part deals with the types of scales used to express pupils' performance. The statistical basis of various scales is described, so that you can appreciate the underlying concepts. Because some fundamental ideas are involved, such as a measured variable, its central point and dispersion, a limited use of statistical notation is introduced.

RAW SCORES

The total figure obtained by adding up the values awarded for each correct response to test questions is known as the 'raw score'. Clearly, a figure on its own is of little consequence. Under certain conditions the pupil's raw score in relation to the maximum for the test might provide enough information for sensible interpretation. For example, a raw score of 24 on a criterion-referenced test with a maximum score of 25 can be confidently accepted as showing almost complete knowledge of, or competence at, the domain tested. However, a more complete understanding can be obtained when other score data are available. For instance, if the score of 24 was obtained by only 1 pupil out of 160 tested, and the next best score was 17, the individual with 24 points would be regarded as exceptional in terms of the test coverage. Other pertinent data might be the *range* of scores, that is, from the lowest score obtained to the highest, say, 15 to 24, a range of 9 points, and an indication of the central score point. A slight difficulty is that there are several different methods for determining the centre of a distribution of pupils' scores, usually referred to as *measures of central tendency*.

The most common measure of central tendency is the average for the group tested. Introducing some notation, in which any pupil's score is denoted by x and the number tested is denoted by n, the total for the group as a whole is Σx, where Σ stands for 'the sum of'; the average or *mean* (to use the statistical term is) is $\Sigma x/n$. Two other central tendency measures are the *mode* and the *median*. The modal score is the one obtained by most people among the group tested. In the example given below, the number of pupils with a score of 17 exceeds the number who obtained any other score in the range, so the mode is 17.

The median is more complicated to explain. Essentially it is the score obtained by the person at the mid-point of the rank order. With 160 pupils in a group, the mid-point is occupied jointly by the eightieth and eighty-first pupils, as illustrated by the imaginary distribution:

Raw score	No. obtaining score	
25	0	
24	1	
23	0	
22	0	
21	0	
20	0	
19	0	
18	0	
17	73	
16	40	80th person is in this score group
15	46	
14 or below	0	
	n =160	

In this example it is obvious that the eightieth pupil is among the group with a score of 16. This distribution shows how we can deal with several ties (more than one person with the same score). First, the score scale is treated as a number line, hence 16 is the integer between 15.5 and 16.5. This unit of score is allocated in even bits to each of the pupils with a score of 16, so hypothetically each of these can be ranked using increments of 1/40. Working from the lowest rank upwards, 46 pupils scored 15, so there are (80−46) pupils to count in order to reach the eightieth individual, that is, 34. (Check: 46 + 34 = 80.) So (34 × 1/40) is the fraction required to locate the 80th pupil up the score scale from 15.5. The value of this fraction is 0.85, hence the 80th person is assumed to have a score of 15.5 + 0.85, that is 16.35.

This exercise can be completed by finding the arithmetic mean for the raw score distribution. The total number of marks (Σx) is readily calculated: 1 pupil with 24 is 24 points; 73 with 17 is 1,241 points; 40 with 16 is 640 points; and 46 with 15 is 690 points. The total comes to 2,595; averaged over 160 pupils this gives 16.22 points per pupil (the mean $\Sigma x/n$, denoted as $\bar{x}$). We can now see that the three measures are fairly close in this example, i.e. mode 17, median 16.35 and mean 16.22.

Test scores for groups should be examined in relation to the distribution of raw scores and one or more central tendency measure. For example, an LEA assessment team had the tests used in a reading survey with Year 5 pupils issued at a feedback meeting. They appreciated the attainment of pupils more fully when they realised that the middle-scoring pupils (near the median) probably answered correctly 23 of the first 44 items in the test (in which the items were broadly graded for complexity). They were also impressed by the variety of questions and the finding that around half of the children knew the answer to, 'He saw the job . . . in the local paper and applied for it'.

Both group results from a test and a single pupil's score are measures of a variable. This general term is used in two ways: first, to define the attribute in respect of which individuals vary (for example the concept of attitude towards enjoyment of science activities); and second, more precisely, to define a metric for the attribute. Users need to have knowledge of the variable, in both senses, to interpret a pupil's score properly.

As a minimum, a measure of a variable is given by its central point and associated dispersion relative to that point. For the mode the appropriate measure of dispersion is the range. For the median a suitable indication of dispersion is the difference on the scale which separates the twenty-fifth and seventy-fifth individuals in a list of 100; in other words, the twenty-fifth and seventy-fifth percentile positions; for example, in a class of 28 pupils the scores of the seventh and twenty-first pupils would give the data required. (*Note:* percentiles are taken in ascending order, higher ranks go with higher scores.)

When the mean is calculated, one measure of dispersion used occasionally is the average deviation. This is the average of the differences between each individual's score and the mean. Clearly, if all the differences above the mean are added up, the total is equal to the sum of all the differences below the mean (taking positive and negative differences together the total sum is zero). When signs are ignored and the differences for each pupil in a distribution are summed and divided by the number in the group, the result is the average of the deviations. The notation for the difference between any pupil's score, x, and the group mean, $\Sigma\bar{x}$, can be written as $(x-\Sigma\bar{x})$. As pointed out above, the algebraic sum of these, when the sign of each difference is taken into account, is zero. In the example below, for 20 pupils with raw scores distributed as shown, the deviations from the mean for each score are those in the last column. The total number of points is 480, and for 20 pupils this gives a mean score of 24.

Raw score scale	No. of pupils	Points per score group	Differences per score group	Total of deviations
30	1	30	$6 \times 1 =$	+6
29	0	0	$5 \times 0 =$	0
28	2	56	$4 \times 2 =$	+8
27	2	54	$3 \times 2 =$	+6
26	0	0	$2 \times 0 =$	0
25	1	25	$1 \times 1 =$	+1
24	5	120	$0 \times 5 =$	0
23	6	138	$-1 \times 6 =$	−6
22	0	0	$-2 \times 0 =$	0
21	1	21	$-3 \times 1 =$	−3
20	1	20	$-4 \times 1 =$	−4
19	0	0	$-5 \times 0 =$	0
18	0	0	$-6 \times 0 =$	0
17	0	0	$-7 \times 0 =$	0
16	1	16	$-8 \times 1 =$	−8

$$n = 20 \qquad \Sigma x = 480$$

$$x = \frac{\Sigma x}{n} = \frac{480}{20} = 24 \qquad \Sigma (x - \bar{x}) = 0$$

In this tidy example the total deviation when signs are disregarded is 42. This gives an average for the 20 pupils of 2.1 points, so we could say that the average deviation on either side of the mean of 24 is 2.1 points. However, a more widely used index of dispersion is the *standard deviation* (SD). There is a statistical reason why the standard deviation is preferred, as will become apparent. The SD is calculated by squaring each pupil's difference from the mean, adding the sum of these squares, averaging the squares' total, then finding the square root of the average. In squaring the deviations all signs become positive, as shown below with the previous data.

Raw score scale	$(x - \bar{x})$	$(x - \bar{x})^2$	No. of pupils in score group	Squared values per score group
30	+6	36	1	36
29	+5	25	0	0
28	+4	16	2	32
27	+3	9	2	18
26	+2	4	0	0
25	+1	1	1	1
24	0	0	5	0
23	−1	1	6	6
22	−2	4	0	0
21	−3	9	1	9
20	−4	16	1	16
19	−5	25	0	0
18	−6	36	0	0
17	−7	49	0	0
16	−8	64	1	64

$$\Sigma(x - \bar{x})^2 = 182$$
(Sum of squares)

$$\frac{\Sigma(x - \bar{x})^2}{n} = \frac{182}{20} = 9.1 \text{ (Mean square or variance)}$$

$$\sqrt{\frac{\Sigma(x - \bar{x})^2}{n}} = \sqrt{9.1} = 3.017 \text{ (SD)}$$

From the raw score data the various measures of dispersion are: range, 30 − 16 = 14 points; inter-quartile range, twenty-fifth to seventy-fifth percentile, that is, fifth to fifteenth pupil up the distribution, 22.5 + 0.33 to 25, that is 22.83 to 25, a difference of 2.17 points; average deviation, 2.1 points; and standard deviation, 3.02 points. The raw score summary for the variable measured by the test is:

mode	23	range	14.00 points
median	23.7	inter-quartile range	2.17 points
mean	24	standard deviation	3.02 points

The main point of the worked example is to show how a measure of central tendency and dispersion convey information which improves score interpretation. For example, a score of 23 or 24 represents average performance, while 26 or better lies in the highest quarter of the range and 21 or lower lies in the lowest quarter. If the test was referenced to a given domain (a course specification with questions sampling each element), the maximum score possible becomes important, as does a zero score. In the case illustrated, no one scored less than 16 points, indicating that no fewer than 16 aspects of the domain had been understood by everyone in the group tested. Views about how much of the domain had been understood by the group would depend on whether the maximum score was 30 or set at a higher point. Obviously teachers who were assessing their pupils' understanding of a unit of curriculum would be pleased had the maximum raw score been 30, and might have been dismayed had it been 100.

Interpretation of raw scores is clarified by showing the distribution graphically. Two representations are given in Figure 1, one with each score group separate, the other with score groups amalgamated in threes and a perpendicular score axis. The convention is to have the score scale along the horizontal axis and pupil numbers counted vertically. Using columns based on score intervals displays the distribution as a histogram. The importance of raw scores is played down in many test manuals when other scales are used; but, as the connection between the test rationale and interpretation stems from the raw score distribution, it is advisable to pay attention to it.

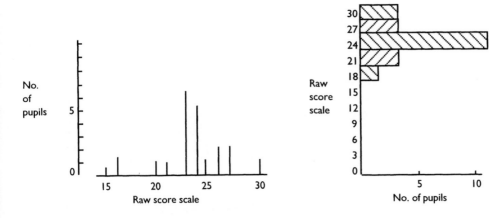

Figure 1 Graphical representation of raw score distribution

PERCENTAGES

Most of us are familiar with transforming a test raw score to another equivalent to assist with its interpretation. The everyday practice of expressing a score as a percentage of the maximum possible value is widely accepted. The simplicity of this method of standardisation arises from the linear relationship between the original scale and its equivalent. This can be illustrated with two number lines.

Raw score scale   0   x/2   x(max)

Percentage scale   0   50   100

The formula to go from any score to a percentage score is $\dfrac{X}{X(max)} \times 100 = P\%$

For example, 8 out of 40 is transformed as follows: $\dfrac{8}{40} \times 100 = 20\%$

Conversely, the formula for finding a raw score from a percentage is:

$\dfrac{P}{100} \times x(max) = x$ For example: $\dfrac{20}{100} \times 40 = 8$

It is useful to think about the meanings commonly attached to percentages. For instance, 50 per cent in an examination usually results in a 'pass'. It seems to denote too that the candidate knew about half of the curriculum dealt with in an examination paper. Also 100 per cent puts an absolute upper limit to performance, while 0 per cent sets an absolute lower limit. Anyone awarded 0 per cent would be seen as knowing nothing about the domain examined. Other vague understandings about percentages are that 65–75 per cent is quite a good standard; 25–35 per cent is really quite poor; 60 per cent is two times better than 30 per cent, and so on.

This latter point is quite intriguing as the relationship can hold good only up to 100 per cent; so what is twice as good a result as 51 per cent? Another widely held idea is that percents can be averaged over two or more results, for example, in a two-part examination with each part carrying equal weight. These comments show that the percentages scale is widely accepted because we believe we understand it. In fact averaging entails adding and then dividing the percentage points, thus treating them as units in a ratio scale, which is not strictly the case. The dispersion of scores for each variable affects the weighting achieved when pupils' scores on two tests are combined (see Part 2B). Disregarding this aspect means that one test result may overwhelm the other(s) when scores are aggregated without due care.

For many criterion-referenced tests, especially those that have a structure built round learning objectives, changing raw scores to percentage marks would obscure the results. But for indicating a performance level relative to implied upper and lower limits, percentages are useful as a standard scale. Percentages should not be used without careful thought, and one pitfall to be avoided is to transform short raw score scales. When this is done, one raw score point difference becomes a large increment as a percentage, a fact which tends to be overlooked when comparisons between individuals are made.

AGE-EQUIVALENT SCALES

The best known version of this type of scale is 'reading age', but others such as 'mental age' are used. One method for determining age-equivalent scores is to calculate mean raw scores for a sequence of age-groups samples. When the means rise progressively, the results are very convincing. The logic in this case is to accept a pupil's score as indicating performance on a par with that of the age-group with a particular mean. For example, the mean raw scores for a mathematics test of 40 items might be:

Age-groups								
(years/months)	8/0	8/3	8/6	8/9	9/0	9/3	9/6	9/9	10/0
mean score	10	14	19	20	22	27	28	29	34

A pupil with a score of 24 would then be allocated an age-equivalent score, by interpolation, of 9 years 1 month.

The other method for determining age-equivalents is to administer trial tests to samples of pupils in different age-groups and then to identify items which are passed (or failed) by half of each group. These items make up the published test. This method was used for some single-word reading tests. The interpretation of results from these is that the highest point (that is, word) reached successfully by a child represents the average attainment of the age-group which corresponds to that point in the test. When each year-group was divided into 12 sub-groups, the 12 words for the year were supposed to represent the median attainment of each monthly sub-population. From the scaling point of view this method is interesting because a pupil's total score is not required; progress through the test up to the point of failure is equated directly with average performance of pupils at a particular age.

Two of the objections to this type of scale are the spurious degree of accuracy which the age equivalence conveys and the lack of information about age-equivalent score distributions for particular populations. The validity of the first objection is shown by the fact that most children do not abruptly reach a failure point in a test with graded items as if they have encountered an insuperable obstacle. Quite the reverse; in most cases pupils fail one or two items, succeed at several more, fail a few, pass one or two and then continue to fail though perhaps with the occasional success. So the tester has to apply a scoring rule of some kind to make a decision about age equivalence. The consequence is that a seemingly exact measure (of attribute age) is being adduced from an approximate measure. Even worse, the implications of any (exact) chronological age versus attribute age discrepancy cannot be truly evaluated. Worse still, seemingly accurate quotients derived from attribute age divided by chronological age multiplied by 100 are used to indicate whether or not performance is in line with expectation.

Of course older children in wide age-range populations generally perform better at a test than younger ones, but their experience and thinking processes are very different too. So the significance of so-called retardation is quite different at various ages, particularly because the development of attributes such as inferential reading does not advance in regular increments as does age.

Teachers who persist with age-equivalent assessments, particularly of reading, should look in the test manuals for any information on the standard error of the reading ages as determined by the test (the standard error concept comes later, in Part 2B), the proportion of children in a given age sub-population who were 6 months, 12 months, 18 months, 24 months, etc., either retarded or advanced, and any reading attainment characteristics ascribed to the various age-equivalents and discrepancies. It is hoped that the lack of information will persuade them to relinquish age-equivalent scales both as a concept and as a measure of development.

CENTILES

Sometimes referred to as 'percentiles', this scale is based on the division of the population into 100 equal parts. The lowest scoring hundredth obtain total raw scores within a certain range at the lowest end of the distribution – and so on for successive hundredths. For example, the twenty-third centile is the point in the raw score scale which marks the upper end of the range spanned by the lowest ranked 23 per cent of the population. It may be necessary to find this score point by interpolation (as for the median) but a whole number approximation is usually accurate enough. The centile points given in some test manuals should be estimated from results obtained from recent, substantial population samples to be accepted as useful norms.

As division into hundredths gives precision that is usually not warranted, sometimes a scale expressed as tenths, called deciles, is used. For example, the seventh decile is the range of scores between the points which divide the lowest sixth-tenths of the population from the upper three-tenths. A pupil scoring in this range would be said to have come within the seventh decile (this would include all of the centiles from 70 to 79).

It is worth noting that centiles and deciles are primarily rank-order scales for comparing a pupil's place within a relevant population, so they are normative. The raw score ranges for each of the deciles will usually not be equal. Also when the overall score distribution on a test is found to be tightly bunched, there will be little real difference in the attribute assessed between adjacent deciles, and the converse applies when the raw score distribution turns out to be widely dispersed. For these and other reasons concerned with the validity of the measure, it is advisable to study closely any information in the test manual on the raw score distributions obtained by the sample(s) from which the norms were obtained.

STANDARDISED SCORES

Any number of procedures for standardising raw scores can be devised, and the percentage conversion is one, familiar method. However, when the term standardised score is used in testing it has a particular meaning, in that the basis for any conversion is the deviation from the mean. Accordingly, data from a sample of pupils are used to calculate deviation units. The standard deviation is regarded as the basic unit, and the scale is laid out on either side of the mean. When the SD is one unit of measurement and the mean (Σx) is assigned a value of zero, the scale line picture is as follows:

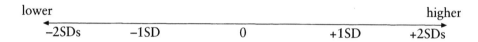

We have to bear in mind that the SD is a form of average representing the dispersion of groups of pupils at different raw score points in relation to the mean. The raw score distribution is unlikely to be symmetrical or even, as Figure 2 indicates.

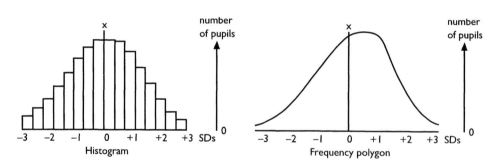

Figure 2: Illustration of asymmetrical raw score distributions

When this form of standardisation is adopted, a pupil's score is expressed as a proportion of an SD above or below the mean. For instance, suppose a test had 100 items each carrying 1 mark and also that the mean for a representative sample of pupils came to 61.3 and the SD was 8.7, then anyone with a score of 61.3+8.7 would have a deviation score of +1, that is, a total of 70 would be equivalent to +1.

Similarly, a score of 45 would have a deviation score of (45–61.3)/8.7 = –1.87 units. It is customary to use z as the symbol for deviation units. As a formula, this reads

$(x–\bar{x})/SD = z$ units of deviation

It is very rare for z to have a value greater than 5. So with a scale range of 5 deviation units on either side of the mean the negative values can be eliminated by adding 5 to every deviation unit. This merely changes the scale to one with a lowest value of 0 to a highest value of 10. In fact the constant used to eliminate the inconvenience of negative signs is chosen arbitrarily, any sensible value will do. For the values given above, –1.87 converts to 3.13 deviation units on a scale with a mean of 5 and an SD of 1.

A further transformation can be done by giving the deviation units any scale suitable equivalent. A common multiple is 10. Combined with the value of 5 used to transpose the mean to a more convenient value, the mean is fixed at a scale point of 50. Hence 3.13 becomes 31.3 on a deviation scale with a mean of 50 and an SD of 10. This scale is very useful for rescaling school exam marks onto a common metric for combining or interpretation (if two raw scores are added together when a group has taken two papers or exams, the set of scores which produced the largest dispersion carries more weight: using the same SD gives equal weights or provides a correct basis for arbitrary differential weights).

Standardisation with deviation unit as the basis can be taken to another dimension by adjusting the distribution to fit the normal probability curve. Imagine a cross-section through a lop-sided jelly, as shown in Figure 3; then imagine that it has been gently pushed to become symmetrical with the bulk piled up towards the middle and the remainder spread towards the sides. Clearly, in a frequency distribution changes which balance the shape could be achieved by shrinking the raw score units under the slope to the left of the first curve and stretching some of those to the right.

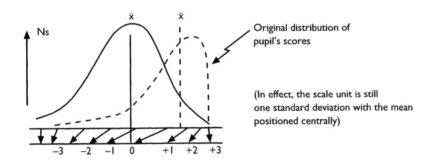

Figure 3: Changes to original scale points due to normalising the distribution

The normal curve model is used because it has features which assist with the interpretation of test scores. The principal one is that the proportions of a population which fall under parts of the curve are known. These proportions are shown in Figure 4 when the baseline is marked off in three ways: (a) in SD units with a mean of zero; (b) with the SD assigned 10 units and mean fixed at 50; and (c) with the SD assigned 15 units and mean fixed at 100.

Figure 4 shows that converting from one normalised scale to another is a very

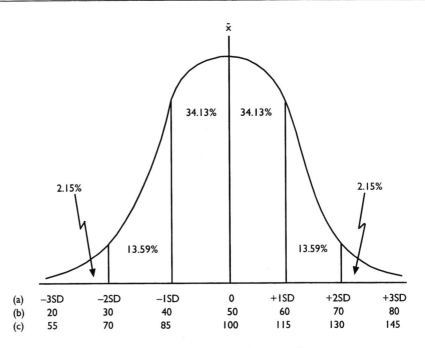

(a)	−3SD	−2SD	−1SD	0	+1SD	+2SD	+3SD
(b)	20	30	40	50	60	70	80
(c)	55	70	85	100	115	130	145

Figure 4: Proportions under normal curve

simple operation. Usually known as the T scale, (b) is a normalised form of the deviation scale described previously and has been used by several test authors (it has a semblance to percentages and might be used with them). However, the predominant convention in psychological and educational testing is scale (c). For example, the graph shows that 50+34.13 = 84.13 per cent of a population is assigned to the score range up to and including 115. At the extremes, only 26 cases in 10,000 would be expected beyond +3SD, that is, below a standardised score of 55 or above one of 145. Also, only the highest 1 per cent of the population would be expected to have scores above 135 on this scale.

There are several misunderstandings about standardisation adjusted to fit the normal curve. One is that all human attributes are distributed among populations 'normally', that is, according to the curve. In fact the raw score distributions on some attribute measures obtained from large representative samples do approach the normal curve. There may be, however, features in the measures which contribute to the way in which the sample is divided. For example, most tests of an ability are composed of questions graded for 'difficulty' on the basis of trials. The consequence is that when a year-group of pupils is tested, there is a hump in the distribution representing the preponderance of middling performers. If measures of certain other attributes are used, the distributions may be very different. For example, when a test of competence at handling money in everyday situations was given to samples of slower learning children in special schools and children in ordinary schools, the scores were comparable and the distributions in both cases were J-shaped, as shown in Figure 5. In this case *the norm* is that most pupils can use money competently. Had the test involved transactions in a foreign language, such as paying for an ice-cream with francs, no doubt the joint distribution would show a different sort of curve, probably a bi-modal (two humps) shape.

The confusion between a norm and the normal distribution is understandable,

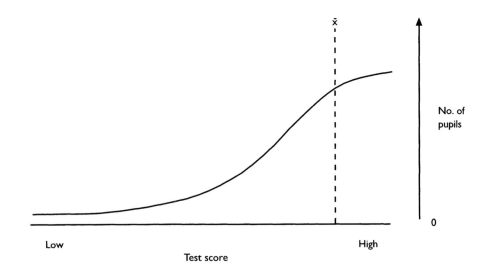

Figure 5: Example of non-normal distribution

especially as the two are often combined in test manuals which have tables of norms for standardised normal scores. It should be kept in mind that a norm essentially describes a social situation. For example, the finding that the majority of children can handle money in everyday situations might be expressed by stating that a score of 62 points (competence criterion) or over on a 70-item test was obtained by 85 per cent of a sample of 12 year olds. There is no particular significance in the score obtained by 50 per cent of the sample or population. The *norms* for such a test would be given by listing the score levels obtained by successive proportions of the sample.

Test manuals which give scores on the conventional standardised scale may also tabulate the score points which approximate the centile divisions. If not, interpretation is aided by reference to tables relating standardised normal scores to centile ranks. Table 13 is given for intervals of 5 points and shows the expected proportions rounded to the nearest whole number, except at the extremes of the range when rounding it to the nearest 0.5. The first column gives the SD, the second the standardised normal scale, the third the proportion of the population up to and including a given score and the fourth the proportion expected within a score interval: for example, the interval between 105 and 110 points includes 12 per cent of the population.

The last column in Table 13 is by far the most important for interpreting standardised normal scores in terms of population norms. It can be seen that just over a quarter of the population would be expected to score within 5 points of the mean of 100; also that a half of the population would score within 10 points of the mean, that is, with scores in the range from 90 to 110. This score bracket can be used to define in a crude way the notion of an average or middling pupil. It also helps a little with the question 'What is an exceptional pupil?' We would probably argue for quite narrow bands, perhaps 9 per cent or maybe 5 per cent. These occur at or above scores of 120 and 125 respectively, and at or below 80 and 75 respectively.

This discussion is relevant to schools' policies and monitoring for pupils deemed to be unusually able or to have exceptional learning difficulties, inevitably

Table 13 Proportions within standardised normal score intervals at certain points

Unit SD	Standardised normal scale point	Percentage of population	Proportion within intervals (%)	Quartiles	
2.33	135	99	1.5		
2.00	130	97.5	2.5		25
1.66	125	95	4.0	24	
1.33	120	91	7.0		
1.00	115	84	9.0		
0.66	110	75	12.0		
0.33	105	63	13.0		
0.00	100	50	13.0	26	50
−0.33	95	37	12.0		
−0.66	90	25	9.0		
−1.00	85	16	7.0		
−1.33	80	9	4.0	24	
−1.66	75	5	2.5		
−2.00	70	2.5	1.5		25
−2.33	65	1			

commented on in Office for Standards in Education (OFSTED) reports. Of course any levels chosen are arbitrary and special needs identification should depend upon a wide range of evidence, test scores included. A further point is that pupils should not be identified as exceptional on one attribute alone and it is, therefore, preferable to appraise the pupils from a number of standpoints rather than rely upon a single indicator such as a test of reasoning ability.

A crucial factor in the interpretation of standardised normal scores is the quality of the norming data. Little reliance can be placed on norms based on inadequate samples, and so the test manual has to be examined for detail with respect to sample representativeness (ideally every pupil in a population could have been chosen as a member), sample size (3,600 is considered adequate for a sample from a year cohort) and age of data (population changes mean that norms lose currency gradually, so that after ten years or so they can be used only tentatively).

Table 14 shows that the score of 100 does not divide the distribution into two equal halves, as might be expected. This is because the scores, notionally, are points on a continuous scoreline. So for example, 100 is the integer corresponding to an interval of 99.5 to 100.5. Accordingly scores of 100 are obtained by a group of individuals. When these are added to all of the other groups with scores below 100, the proportion of the population comes to 51.3. Bearing in mind that the standard normal scores are transformations from unit raw scores, and that any score has a probability of error, pupils' centile positions should be taken as approximate, for example, a pupil with a score of 80 would be at or near the tenth centile.

STANDARDISED AGE SCORES

When a variable is found to be influenced by age, it is useful on occasions to have a scale which incorporates an age allowance. Age effects are detected by organising the scores from different age-groups as separate distributions. If, say, 3,600 pupils

Table 14: Table for converting standardised scores to percentiles

Standardised score	Percentile	Standardised score	Percentile	Standardised score	Percentile	Standardised score	Percentile
140	99.7	120	91.4	100	51.3	80	9.7
139	99.6	119	90.3	99	48.7	79	8.6
138	99.5	118	89.1	98	46.0	78	7.6
137	99.4	117	87.8	97	43.4	77	6.7
136	99.3	116	86.4	96	40.8	76	5.9
135	99.1	115	84.9	95	38.2	75	5.1
134	98.9	114	83.3	94	35.7	74	4.5
133	98.7	113	81.6	93	33.3	73	3.9
132	98.5	112	79.7	92	30.9	72	3.3
131	98.2	111	77.8	91	28.5	71	2.9
130	97.9	110	75.0	90	26.3	70	2.5
129	97.5	109	73.7	89	24.2		
128	97.1	108	71.5	88	22.2		
127	96.7	107	69.1	87	20.3		
126	96.1	106	66.7	86	18.4		
125	95.5	105	64.3	85	16.7		
124	94.9	104	61.8	84	15.1		
123	94.1	103	59.2	83	13.6		
122	93.3	102	56.6	82	12.2		

from a year cohort are sampled, there will be about 300 in each month. Any age effect shows in the means for each month group. For example, if a September 8 year old's sample is tested in February, the youngest member would be 8 years 6 months and the oldest would be almost 9 years 5 months. If the mean test raw score is found to rise gradually across the month groups, there is a cross-sectional age effect. A difference of, say, 6 raw score points across the 12 months means that the older pupils tend to have had an advantage. In the norms, this is nullified by setting the mean for each month group to 100 and normalising the raw score distributions for each month group.

The result is that differences between pupils' standardised scores due to age are controlled, thus enabling the results for pupils tested at the same time to be compared. Usually test manuals have tables for standardised age scores. Often these are printed in month by month columns, but there are some tests with scores for three-monthly groups and others where the user has to add a given constant to younger pupils' scores when converting raw scores to standardised ones.

The adjustments described above do not take into account the tendency for all pupils to obtain higher scores on a test if it is taken later rather than earlier in their lives. Strictly speaking, test authors or publishers should carry out one or more cross-sectional standardisations at different times of the year if their tests are likely to be used at various times. For example, tests standardised at about the middle of each term will have adequate information on both cross-sectional and longitudinal age variations for reasonably accurate age adjustments to be given.

However, it has to be said that the fine corrections to standardised scores often given in test tables convey an unwarranted impression of accuracy. There may also be problems when a test is given to a run of year-groups. These usually attain progressively higher mean scores. At the same time, there will be large proportions of pupils within the extreme year-groups who obtain either very high or very low scores. These raw score distributions will be skewed, as shown in Figure 6. In

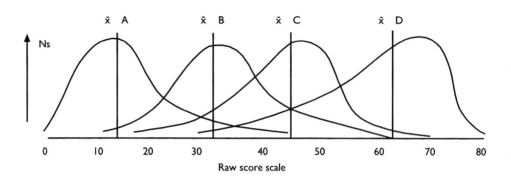

Figure 6: Raw score distributions for successive year groups given a single test

addition, the year-groups in the middle of the range will tend to be compressed into a narrow raw score range.

Normalisation of each of these distributions will change the shape of groups A and D more than for groups B and C. Consequently, the age compensation is uneven within year-groups. Teachers have been baffled to find children with adjacent raw scores who are a few months different in age allocated markedly different standardised scores. This result is highly unsatisfactory as it is an artefact of the statistical procedures. Therefore it is preferable to use a test specifically designed for the age-group concerned. Test users should inspect the standardised age score tables for wide age-range tests to see whether the effects described above are apparent. If they are, then the test should not be used for pupils in the age-groups affected.

Stanines and Stens

Stanines and stens are divisions of the standardised normal scale chosen to indicate a pupil's approximate position in a population in a readily interpreted way. Both scales have a base unit of one-half of a standard deviation. The difference is that stanines have a middle unit which spans the mean; stens have a mid-point at the mean. The labels are contractions of 'standard nines' and 'standard tens' respectively. The tails of a normal distribution stretch towards infinity so the divisions at the end of both scales are not true units, as indicated in Table 15.

The stanine scale is quite widely used for reporting test results. Its interpretation should be normative; for instance, a pupil in the third stanine is one whose test performance places him/her among the 12.1 per cent whose results were better than the lowest 10.6 per cent of the population. Stens are less widely used. Compared with stanines, the scale gives more discrimination at the extremes but a disadvantage is that the pupils in the middle of the range are not differentiated as sharply (Figure 7).

One justification for using these scales is the approximate nature of test raw scores. Standardised normal scores, like all other measurements, have a degree of error, as discussed in Part 2B. But the same point applies to classification into stanines or stens. Some pupils allocated a sten of 8 may truly have been a 7 or 9; in other words, 8 is the notional mid-point of a bracket of scale values (7, 8, 9) and, but for error, they would have been just into the range of the seventh or ninth sten or stanine.

Test authors who favour the use of stanines because they provide a better form of report, to be seen by parents and discussed with them, should remind users that the

Table 15 Score points and distributions for populations in stanines and stens

	Stanines				Stens			
Unit SDs	Stanine	x̄ SD 100,15	Percentage in range	Cumulative percentage	Unit SDs	Sten	x̄ SD 100,15	Percentage in range	Cumulative percentage
	9		4.0	100		10		2.3	100
+1.75		126.25			+2.0		130		
	8		6.6	96.4		9		4.4	97.7
+1.25		118.75			+1.5		122.5		
	7		12.1	89.8		8		9.2	93.3
+0.75		111.25			+1.0		115		
	6		17.5	77.7		7		14.9	84.1
+0.25		103.75			+0.5		107.5		
	5		19.7	60.2		6		19.2	69.2
−0.25		96.25			0.0		100		
	4		17.5	40.5		5		19.2	50
−0.75		88.75			−0.5		92.5		
	3		12.1	22.7		4		14.9	30.8
−1.25		81.25			−1.0		85		
	2		6.6	10.6		3		9.2	15.9
−1.75		73.75			−1.5		77.5		
	1		4.0	4.0		2		4.4	6.7
					−1.0		70		
						1		2.3	2.3

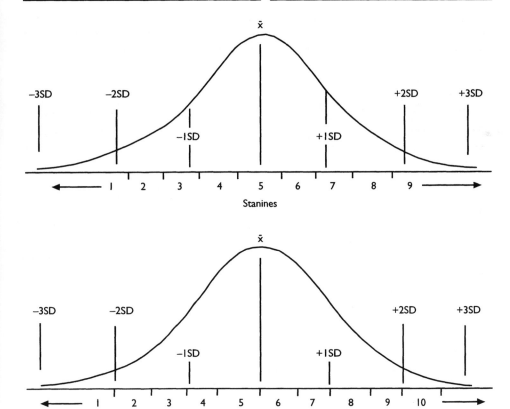

Figure 7: Stanines and stens in relation to the normal curve

scale condenses a much wider range of scores into one represented by nine numerals. Furthermore, each numeral shows a rank order of pupils grouped into equal score bands; however, these bands contain different proportions of the population, with rather more than a half falling within the three middle bands of 4, 5 and 6.

Grades

The same argument about approximation underlies the use of broad grades or levels. One series of reasoning tests employs a five-grade classification which divides the population into successive bands of 10, 20, 40, 20 and 10 per cent, labelled grades A to E respectively. These divisions are made on the basis of raw scores. It is worth noting that these arbitrary groupings are often justified as 'based on the normal curve'. The standardised normal score points ($\Sigma x=100$, SD=15) which divide these categories are E/D, 82.8; D/C, 92.2; C/B, 107.8; B/A, 119.2. Rounded to the nearest whole number these values are 81, 93, 108, 119.

The problem with this type of classification is that it is really too crude. For example, a pupil's raw score could occur near to the point equivalent to a standardised normal score of 93. If the pupil's score leads to a C-grade allocation, the user would have no indication that his/her performance was borderline with D grade; the best interpretation that can be given to C grade is 'about average', that is, near the middle of the middle 40 per cent. Clearly, this interpretation would be quite misleading. On occasions, these grades are recommended for reporting test results to parents. The best point in favour is that only 30 per cent of the parents (of an 'average' group) have to be told that their son or daughter is 'below average'!

Other Types of Scale: Longitudinal

There is a tendency for tests in Britain to follow trends in the USA, where pupils are tested more extensively during their school and college careers. Rather than promote single tests for specific applications, publishers are producing various series for successive age-groups. Within each series there are usually several sub-tests or separate tests, each scored in the same manner (usually by machine-read score sheets) and scaled in the same way.

Sometimes the test questions are printed in a single booklet containing instructions to pupils about the level to be attempted and, in particular, the starting points for each age-group. The manuals for these tests may contain a scale which connects the results for the whole series. At its most basic this scale could comprise the overall raw score total for all the tests accumulated age-group by age-group. For instance, if six age levels are each to attempt 40 items in a vocabulary sub-test, the sequence of items for age-groups might be:

Level	Group		Start		Finish
A	Year 2	items	1	to	40
B	Year 3	items	21	to	60
C	Year 4	items	41	to	80
D	Year 5	items	61	to	100
E	Year 6	items	81	to	120
F	Year 7	items	101	to	140

Here the overall raw score scale would be 140, but a Year 3 pupil top-scorer could obtain only a maximum of 80; however, all children in this age band would be credited initially with 40 points. Such a scheme could be adopted only when adequate sample trials had verified the overlaps between score bands. However, slow-learning pupils, or the very advanced, could start at a lower or higher level, as appropriate. Results from these pupils would be included in the standardisations for the age-groups.

There are numerous methods for creating longitudinal scales and as many labels for them, for example, the 'universal scale'. When the origin of a scale is age-group data, interpretation is via norm comparisons; when the basis is a curriculum, interpretation reflects the pupil's standard of performance by curriculum elements understood. SATs are a crude version of a longitudinal scale: there is no overlapping design, merely arbitrary 'expected' levels based on age-related curricula.

Item Response

The overlapping design, illustrated above, would be acceptable only if samples of pupils from the successive age-groups performed consistently at the sets of 20 items which make up the two halves of each level test (except for A and F). For example, Year 4 pupils would have items 40–60 in common with Year 5. Presumably these questions would be relatively hard for the Year 4 children and relatively easy for Year 5 children. 'Easiness' or 'difficulty' would be apparent from proportions in the trial samples giving correct answers (item 'facility values'). So for item 41, the Year 4 result might be 60 per cent correct, while for Year 5 this might be 80 per cent correct. Consider another item, say number 60: if 15 per cent of Year 4 pupils give a correct answer, what percentage would we expect from the Year 5 sample?

It is assumed that the dimensions in the variable underlying pupils' responses are the same for both age-groups. From the data the ratio of Year 4 pupils responding correctly to items 41 and 60 is 4:1; also the inter-year ratio for item 41 is 3:4; hence the response level expected for Year 3 pupils to item 60 is 20 per cent.

When the data from trials of test items consistently fit patterns of the kind illustrated, the hypotheses about dimensionality and attribute make-up are supported. The difficulties for the test constructor are the approximate values given by trial data and the need to evaluate the hypotheses a variety of contexts, for example, by comparing high-scoring group results with low-scoring groups of the same age, and by repeating the trials with independent samples of pupils. Given these conditions are met, substantial sets of questions can be built up and linked together on a single scale.

The main point of the illustration is to show that the relative difficulties of items (as shown by samples of facility values) can be used to scale items on the basis of the response probabilities. Also large numbers of items can be scaled by linking one trial set with others using overlapping designs. A result is that banks or pools of items can be established, which can be used to 'tailor' efficient tests for specific applications. Schools may have educational psychologists assessing some pupils with the British Ability Scales, and these have been standardised using relative difficulty scales.

Part 2B
Handling Test Data

In this part we aim to encourage schools and teachers to use test data descriptively and to look critically at the results and their implications. Several related notions are involved, all stemming from the idea that a test variable distribution can be expressed as the arithmetic mean, with each pupil's score deviating from it by a particular amount. Also, that classes or other pupil groupings are population samples and test results are the product of one-off occasions affected by a range of factors. These affect both individuals and the sample as a whole and so influence the group overall performance.

To illustrate this point, imagine that several children were asked to measure a length of wrinkled cloth. Some would standardise the conditions by ironing the cloth, others would try stretching it out; some would use the tape carefully, others would make mistakes in reading the scale. It might not be possible to measure an exact length, but it is highly likely that the best estimate of a 'true' length would be the average of those made by the children. By doing so, individual pupils' errors are assumed to have been evened out. We might also find that the averages obtained by other groups were fairly similar or quite different. We can see that the likely amount of individual errors, and their effect on the group mean, should be examined when results are interpreted.

The term used to indicate the probable spread of error in estimates is 'standard error'. This general term refers to the estimated standard deviation of certain measures. For group means this SD is called the *standard error of the mean*; for individual scores it is the *standard error of score*. As the 'errors' tend to be normally distributed, the curve's features are used to define conventional limits which assist with deciding whether or not the inherent variability in the results makes decision-taking defensible.

Some teachers make use of the techniques outlined in this chapter. But often pupils are assessed and their results listed with no follow-up analysis done. For commercial tests, computer scoring systems usually provide some of the information such as group sub-test means and the standard errors for these. While such statistics are important, by themselves they are of limited use for monitoring and setting targets. Additional analyses are usually needed, such as comparisons of different tests results.

An example concerns Year 5 tests given as part of an LEA 'screening' procedure. A school headteacher customarily administered the two tests sent by the authority and marked the scripts. The teachers were then told who the low-scoring children were. Usually there were no surprises, but the teachers were quite depressed to find how far down the scale the slower children came and were not encouraged by the head's remarks about 'children who are falling behind'. One year the class means were calculated. For one it was found that the mean for the mathematics test was about 108, and the mean for reading was about 106. As these results were somewhat higher than the means for the LEA, the teacher's view of the class (and the tests) was transformed.

GRAPHIC REPRESENTATION

Test data for groups are more readily appreciated when their distribution is shown graphically. The procedure basically consists of counting the frequency with which each score occurs among the sample of pupils. It is usually preferable to group scores into class intervals. One method is to peruse the list of scores to find the range. Say that the 30 pupils in the class had obtained a range from 21 to 54 (33 points); this number of pupils and the range suggests a class interval of 5 points. A hand tally by class intervals might look like this:

21 – 25	26 – 30	31 – 35	36 – 40	41 – 45	46 – 50	51 – 55
///	//	////	ЦНГ //	ЦНГ /	ЦНГ	///
3	2	4	7	6	5	3

These data could be portrayed as a histogram or as a frequency polygon, shown in Figure 8.

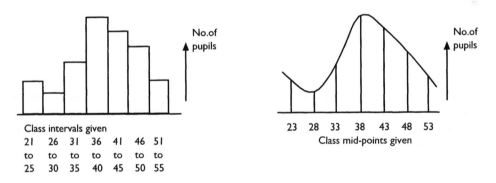

Figure 8 Examples of frequency distributions shown by histogram and frequency polygon

The histogram base in Figure 8 is set out in fives, whereas the frequency polygon base is set out to show the mid-point of each class interval. Some statistics computer programs offer a variety of graphs and determine the base divisions. For class teachers there is some advantage in drawing the graphs by hand as this procedure brings home the position achieved by each pupil among the group. For the national testing levels, instead of class intervals the baseline shows each level administered for each subject.

MEAN, STANDARD DEVIATION AND STANDARD ERROR OF THE MEAN

In the case of the screening test results, referred to earlier, the mathematics and reading test class means were about 8 and 6 points respectively above the standardisation population means of 100. This information gave the teacher a different view of the class, especially when it was pointed out that the means for the LEA population of 7,000 or so pupils were also higher than the standardised means by almost 5 points, for both tests.

In fact the class happened to be quite close to the LEA means. But even had the means been quite a few points different, there would probably have been grounds for accepting that the results were merely part of the general run of events, in which case there would be no cause for the teacher to be worried. The reason is that sub-samples within a population can be expected to vary quite markedly.

Consider that the (population) standardisation sample raw score result and the LEA raw score result had produced mean scores of 100 and about 105 respectively. The five-point difference would be significant because both results came from large numbers. But each of these groups would be made up of many classes of pupils from a large number of schools, each class being a sub-sample. These separate sub-samples would each produce a mean, so there is a distribution of means created in both the national standardisation exercise and the LEA survey. The *distribution of means* from samples tend to pile up around the relevant population mean; indeed the distribution of means tends to be normal in shape (and degree of dispersion is indicated by a standard deviation value).

To distinguish the dispersion of sample means (for a given size of sample) from the dispersion that applies to a set of individuals' scores the term standard error of the mean is used (written as SE_m). In the case of the LEA, the SE_m can be found by computing the obtained SD divided by the square root of the number of pupils. For instance, with an SD of 13, say,

$$SE_m = \frac{SD}{\sqrt{N}} = \frac{13}{\sqrt{7000}} = \frac{13}{83.67} = 0.155$$

(Compared with the population SD of 13, the value of 0.155 is relatively small.)

The SE_m of a sub-sample mean can be estimated from a similar formula, that is, the SD divided by the square root of the number of pupils minus one. Say the SD for one teacher's class of 35 pupils was 8.5, the SE_m of the class mean is estimated from

$$SE_m = \frac{8.5}{\sqrt{34}} = \frac{8.5}{5.83} = 1.46$$

(a relatively large value). This latter value shows that the SD for the distribution of means for samples of this size is estimated to be 1.46. One SD on both sides of the mean encompasses a range of ±1.46, that is, 2.92 points. The scale value of the SE_m range is applied to produce a *confidence interval*, as explained below.

To recapitulate, different proportions of a sample of normally distributed values are related to corresponding areas under the normal curve. So plus and minus $1SE_m$ for a distribution of means encompasses 68 per cent of cases, that is, there is a 68 per cent probability that a sample of size N would have a mean in this confidence interval. A larger interval or band can be obtained by accepting a higher probability;

for example, plus and minus 2SE$_m$ would give a 96 per cent level of probability (meaning that for samples of size N there is a 96 per cent probability that the mean for any sample will fall within the confidence interval given by ±2SE$_m$). Conventionally two confidence limits are used, one at 95 and the other at 99 per cent. The former has 1.96 standard error values, while the latter has 2.58 standard error values. These confidence limits are often referred to, alternatively, as the 5 and 1 per cent levels of significance (Figure 9).

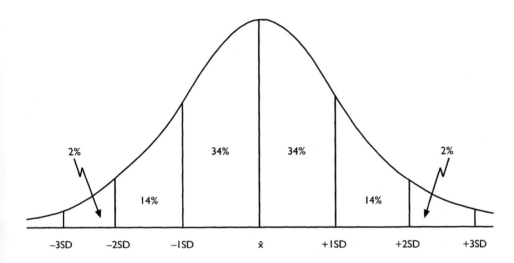

Figure 9 Area under the normal curve by deviation units

The meaning of these two levels of significance is stated in terms of probabilities. For the narrower confidence interval there is a 1 in 20 chance that the sample mean obtained is not a member of the population of means for randomly drawn samples of the same size. For the wider confidence band the probability that the sample mean is not a member of the same population is 1 in 100. Put the other way round, the odds respectively are 19 to 1 and 99 to 1 that when a mean value lies within a confidence band there is no significant difference between the sample and the parent population.

To compare a teacher's class mean for reading scores of 106 with the LEA population mean of 105 entails finding the difference between the means (in this case 1 point) and comparing this with the standard error applied to a confidence interval. With SE$_m$ = 1.46, there is no need to consider the 5 and 1 per cent levels because the difference of one point is obviously smaller than the standard error of the mean.

However, suppose the class mean had been as low as 102 points. The difference from the LEA mean of 105 is three points. The two significance levels give rise to confidence bands of 1.46 × 1.96 = 2.86 at 5 per cent, and 1.46 × 2.58 = 3.77 at 1 per cent. Clearly, only one of these values is less than the difference between the means of three points, so this difference can be regarded as statistically significant beyond the 5 per cent level of significance, but not up to the 1 per cent level. Expressed another way, we could say that there is somewhat higher than 1 chance in 20 that this class difference of three points below the county mean arose from chance effects.

Compared with the standardisation (population) mean of 100, a sub-sample mean which differs by more than the 2.86 points of the 95 per cent confidence band could be regarded as interesting. So we might decide to set upper and lower limits of 100 + 2.86 and look only at classes whose means fall above 102.86 or below 97.14.

The principle which operates when groups are being compared is that larger samples (from a population) produce more certainty with regard to estimating the population mean. The formula used earlier on has square root of the sample size minus one in the denominator; the standard error is thus reduced in proportion to the square of the sample numbers. Thus to halve the standard error of the mean obtained from a sample of size N by enlarging the sample entails quadrupling the sample size. For a sample of 101 pupils (N–1) = 10, so that the SE_m is 10 per cent of the SD for the sample. For a sample of 401 pupils, $\sqrt{(N–1)} = 20$; for a sample of 1,601 pupils $\sqrt{(N–1)} = 40$. Towards the other extreme, for 26 pupils, $\sqrt{(N–1)} = 5$.

The implications of this arithmetic are that comparisons between small samples and very large LEA population or standardisation sample means are unlikely to show significant differences at even the lower level of significance (5 per cent) unless the sample SD is also relatively very small. This situation can occur when there is a concentration of pupils' score at or near the same standard (and therefore little deviation from the sample mean). Much of this is common sense.

In the case of the teacher whose attention was directed to the lower-attaining pupils, calculation of the class means (as if the pupils were a random sample) was extremely reassuring. And even if the means for the class had been significantly different at one or other level of significance, there would have been strong educational inferences to be drawn. For example, had the difference between the LEA mean and the class mean been relatively large, the class might have been regarded as exceptional. A significantly lower than LEA mean (beyond the 1 per cent level) could have implied that additional support for the teacher and children should be considered, as monitoring without support when warranted is a waste of time. A significantly higher than LEA mean might have implied that the reading curriculum aims and content should be revised and possibly, less time given to it.

While computer programs instantly provide the mean and SD of a score distribution, it may be necessary to calculate the SE_m by hand (with an electronic calculator). If you have class lists of test or examination scores on computer file, it would be a useful exercise to find the mean, SD and SE_m for one or more sets of scores. The values should then be multiplied by 1.96 to give the 5 per cent confidence interval for each variable. Assuming that the population mean is 100 or a comparable figure for another scale, decide whether each difference from the standard mean is significant at the 5 per cent level of confidence.

Note: There is a distinction between educational significance and statistical significance. The latter is useful for deciding whether to take a result seriously in cases where it is not fairly obvious from the data. In the example given above, a class mean of 115, say, would have made a statistical significance test superfluous.

INTERPRETING INDIVIDUAL SCORES

The idea that a test score or grade is an estimate of a pupil's position on a scale which represents a variable has been stressed previously. How good an estimate it is depends on certain qualities inherent in each test or assessment. These qualities relate to how well the measure represents the attribute under consideration and also whether the measure obtained is unbiased or the product of an erratic instrument. This section deals with the measure as an accurate and reliable instrument of assessment.

The two concepts can be separated, as a mundane illustration tells: a vintage car petrol gauge shows 'full' when the tank is topped up to overflowing and 'empty' when about half the fuel has been used. The gauge is not accurate, but it is reliable. In other words, it is systematically biased but consistent in different places and on different days; the measure is repeatable. Despite its lack of precision, the car's drivers find the estimate given by the gauge useful because they can reliably estimate the 'true' measure of petrol in the tank (and they keep a reserve can of petrol in the boot).

In testing, three concepts of reliability have been developed. One is internal consistency (the extent to which the test items each contribute towards the total score); the second is equivalence (the extent to which different tests of the same attribute produce comparable scores for the same pupils); and the third is stability (the extent to which total scores are replicated if pupils are tested on two separate occasions).

If a test is not internally consistent, the implication is that some of the items can be answered by drawing on other attributes than the one which is the object of the test. In this case, the test lacks homogeneity. In fact it is the inconsistency between individuals who take the test which gives rise to its unreliability. For instance, if two people both scored 50 on a 100-item test of historical events, but both answered different questions correctly, their results could hardly be regarded as comparable. If many other pupils obtained scores in a similar way, the test as a whole would be regarded as producing internally inconsistent results.

Equivalence between two tests of the same attribute would be demonstrated if a list of pupils' scores on both tests gave much the same rank orders. Correlation is shown by the symbol r, and between the two variables A and B, the symbol format is r_{AB}. When the two score lists for a set of pupils correspond exactly r has a maximum value of 1.0. If the ranks are inversely related (that is, the top pupil on one test is bottom on the other, the middle pupil is middle on both, and so on), the value of r is −1.0. Higgledy-piggledy rank pairs produce a value for r of about 0. In fact correlations can be computed from the test scores without the need to produce rank orders.

Two tests can be made 'parallel' to the extent of having the same content areas, structure and number of items (theoretically items are interchangeable between tests). Such a deliberate attempt to create equivalence might be expected to yield values of r which approach the maximum of 1.0. In fact 'parallel form' correlations of around 0.9 are more usual, partly because the two tests are taken by the same pupils on different occasions (performance varies due to time as well as content).

The time problem also besets the estimation of stability in test results, known as 'test re-test reliability'. If children are given the test for a second time immediately after the first administration, they are likely to recall many of their responses and also benefit from practice. But if the re-test is delayed considerably, their performance might well improve because of genuine learning, though some may progress more than others. In practice, stability coefficients are obtained from test administrations between one and six weeks apart. In many cases, coefficients of r can exceed 0.9.

Of course, if scoring involves judges in interpreting mark keys or other assessment criteria, as in written school examinations or national tests, there is likely to be less equivalence between test versions or consistency between the parts of a test or stability over time. This means that an individual pupil's score might fluctuate because of differences between judges (when more than one marks a set of scripts) or inconsistency on the part of single judges. When groups of assessors meet to discuss their application of mark schemes or criteria in so called moderation meetings, they are attempting to make their judgements equivalent. An aspect which is seldom addressed explicitly, though it should be, is the equivalence of standards over time when different tasks or test papers are given to successive populations of pupils year after year, as in National Curriculum assessments or external examinations. (Sub-samples could be given samples of tasks given in previous years to estimate the variation due to tasks, but this would require more time, money and planning.) Teachers might well 'recycle' items (questions and score keys) or reuse whole tests with successive year-groups as part of their monitoring. They could also challenge assessment bodies to give information about the reliability of grades, grade boundaries and assessors.

Common sense tells us that when a test result derives from an unreliable test, the score is only an approximation of that which would have been obtained had a perfectly reliable test been used. The question, then, is what range of score is it reasonable to take as the band within which the 'true' score would have occurred. There are many ways of estimating the size of this band, though the choice of the reliability coefficient used in the calculation can have a substantial effect. Once again, the concept of a sample of results normally distributed is useful. The reason is that the standard deviation of such a hypothetical distribution of test scores is taken to give an index called the standard error of score, SE_{score}.

Relevant formula
Standard deviation from a population or sample multiplied by the square root of 1 minus the reliability coefficient.

$$SE_{score} = SD \sqrt{(1-r_{AB})}$$

In this formula r_{AB} is the estimated reliability coefficient obtained from correlating two parallel forms of a test, A and B (other types of reliability coefficients are used, but it is not necessary to cite these formulae here).

Worked example
Given that the test standardisation SD = 15 and test re-test r = 0.84

$$\begin{aligned}
SE_{score} &= \sqrt{(1-0.84)} \\
&= 15 \sqrt{0.16} \\
&= 15 \times 0.4 \\
&= 6.0 \text{ points}
\end{aligned}$$

Interpretation
This standard error implies that we can be confident, with odds of 68 to 32, that a pupil's 'true' score would fall within a band of plus and minus one standard errors, that is, 12 points. This band is applied to the score obtained by anyone taking the

test. Thus a pupil who obtained, say, 92 would have a confidence band of plus and minus one standard error between 86 and 98. As would be expected, a wider band gives even more confidence that the range captures the 'true' score. Thus at the 95 per cent confidence limits the band would be $1.96 \times 6 = 11.76$ points on either side of an obtained score, and for the 1 per cent limits the range would be twice $2.58 \times 6 = 2 \times 15.48 = 30.96$. This figure implies that a pupil who obtained a score in excess of 115 is hardly likely to be average (have a 'true' score at the mean) as the odds are about 99 to 1 against.

The main point of the foregoing discussion is to underline the approximate nature of the score obtained by a pupil and, correspondingly, to emphasise the importance of using tests or other forms of assessment which have been made as reliable as possible by their authors. Test manuals ought to give appropriate reliability data (sample sizes, school and demographic details) and the type(s) of any coefficient(s) calculated. Furthermore, the user should find clear statements of the standard error of score and, ideally, illustrations showing the range of scores associated with certain confidence levels. There are many procedures and formulae for estimating test reliability, which differ according to type, that is, internal consistency, equivalence or stability. Figure 10 illustrates how a pupil's scores can be recorded to show the confidence band.

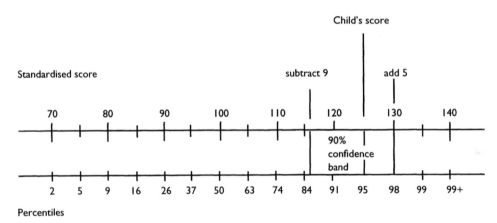

Figure 10 Example of recording a pupil's score on a standardised scale within a confidence band

The preceding discussion has shown that treating test scores as precise measures is not sound practice. Thus comments, for instance, that a child scoring 99 on a standardised reading test, as compared with a previous (and different test) score of 104, has fallen below average can be seen to be nonsensical. A five-point difference would be something like the standard error of score associated with results for both tests. By thinking along the lines that both results are each a sample taken from a distribution with an SD of about 5 it can be appreciated that the results might well have overlapped considerably.

In the absence of a calculated reliability coefficient for a school test, it is suggested that you might use a moderately high figure (say 0.85) in conjunction with the obtained SD to estimate the standard error (SE) of score on a 'test' for a class or year group. Then calculate the confidence intervals for ±1SE for the 5 per cent level of significance (that is 1SE × 1.96) and round the results up to the nearest whole number. Run down the class list and asterisk any pupil whose score lies further from the mean than this value. When looking at a string of results from a pupil, it is useful to keep this range of possible variation in mind. Should results fall outside this bracket, pupils might be asked for their views on the targets they have in mind.

COMPARING TWO GROUPS OF PUPILS

When two separate groups of pupils take the same test, you can compare the means for each group by treating them as random samples from the same population. Had this been the case, you would anticipate that the means would be similar. Of course a few large differences might occur because of chance (for example, guessing multiple-choice answers, more children disliking the test situation in one group, and so on).

The procedure with two groups to compare is, first, to calculate the respective group mean, SD and SE_m, then to apply the formula for the standard error of the difference between means. The result is an estimate of the standard deviation for a distribution of differences between means for samples of the sizes achieved. Using the normal curve model once again, the confidence intervals for evaluating differences of certain magnitudes can be found by forming what is termed a critical ratio (CR).

Relevant formula

$SEdiff_{1,2} = \sqrt{[(SE_{m1})^2 + (SE_{m2})^2]}$ The standard error of the difference between means is the square root of the sum of the squared standard error of the means for both groups.

Critical ratio, $CR = \dfrac{Diff_{1,2}}{SEdiff_{1,2}}$ Difference between the group means, divided by the standard error of the difference.

Worked example

Evaluate the difference between two successive year-groups of pupils, groups 1 and 2, who obtained standardised mean scores of 98 and 102. There are 122 and 145 pupils respectively in the groups; the SDs were 10 and 14. First, find the standard error of the means (SE_ms) for both groups:

$$SE_{m1} = \frac{10}{\sqrt{(122-1)}} = \frac{10}{\sqrt{121}} = \frac{10}{11} = 0.91$$

$$SE_{m2} = \frac{14}{\sqrt{(145-1)}} = \frac{14}{\sqrt{144}} = \frac{14}{12} = 1.17$$

In the formula $SEdiff_{1,2} = \sqrt{(0.91^2 + 1.17^2)}$
$$= \sqrt{2.19}$$
$$= 1.48$$

Then form a critical ratio:

$$CR = \frac{102 - 98}{1.48} = \frac{4}{1.48} = 2.70$$

Interpretation

Hypothetically two groups chosen at random from a population would have the same mean, that is, the difference between means would be zero. But a difference can be anticipated due to chance factors. With a value of 2.70, the CR exceeds the significance level for 99 per cent of cases, that is, a value of 2.58. In this case we can regard the difference of four points as highly significant.

The t-ratio

When the two groups to be compared are small (less than 30 is the usual limit), it is necessary to use an adjusted critical ratio set of values, known as the t-distribution. Computer programs for evaluating differences between means usually have the t-distributions incorporated, but it is as well to check, otherwise any small group comparisons could be misleading. The formula for calculating the value of t for two samples which differ in size is:

$$t = \frac{M_1 - M_2}{\sqrt{\left[\dfrac{\Sigma(x_1 - \bar{x}_1)^2 + \Sigma(x_2 - \bar{x}_2)^2}{N_1 + N_2 - 2} \times \dfrac{N_1 + N_2}{N_1 N_2} \right]}}$$

You may recognise the terms in each bracket of the denominator as the sums of the squared deviations for the respective variables, usually referred to as the 'sum of squares' (found by squaring the SD and multiplying by the group size); t is evaluated according to the 'degrees of freedom' which samples of the size N_1 and N_2 have to vary, that is, $N_1 + N_2 - 2$ (the combined samples minus two). The idea behind degrees of freedom is that with any pupil in a distribution taken as a reference-point, there are $N - 1$ variations from it which are possible.

Reworking the example used above, but with class sizes of 30 and 24 and test score SDs of 8 and 6.5 (smaller groups usually have relatively smaller score dispersions), illustrates how the difference between means of 98 and 102 should be interpreted. First, we need to find the 'sum of squares' to give values for both $(x - \bar{x})^2$ terms.

For the first test this is $8^2 \times 30 = 1920$. For the other it is $6.5^2 \times 24 = 1020$.

Using these values, class sizes and means to find t:

$$t = \frac{102 - 98}{\sqrt{\left(\dfrac{1920 + 1020}{30 + 24 - 2} \times \dfrac{30 + 24}{30 \times 24} \right)}}$$

$$= \frac{4}{\sqrt{\left(\dfrac{2940}{52} \times \dfrac{54}{720} \right)}}$$

$$= \frac{4}{\sqrt{(56.54 \times 0.075)}} = \frac{4}{\sqrt{4.24}} = \frac{4}{2.06} = 1.94$$

As t has a value slightly lower than 2.01, the 5 per cent confidence value of t for 50 degrees of freedom given in the statistical table of t, the difference of four points may be regarded as attributable to chance variation. In other words, the four-point difference is not significant at the 5 per cent level of confidence. We can see once more from these examples that group size is a critical factor when group means are compared.

Difference between Means for Correlated Scores

A different case has to be considered if we compare the same group of pupils for their performance on two variables. The reason is that the scores are probably correlated, and this affects the conclusions to be drawn from a difference between the means. Accordingly, it is necessary to calculate the correlation between the variables.

Relevant formula
For variables labelled A and B

$$SE_{diff,AB\ corr} = \sqrt{[(SE_{mA})^2 + (SE_{mB})^2 - 2r.SE_{mA}.SE_{mB}]}$$

that is the square root of the sum of the SE_m for both tests, minus twice the product of the correlation coefficient and the standard errors.

Worked example
Imagine that a class of 26 pupils produced data as follows:

Test A mean 93; SD = 7   Test B mean 99: SD = 5.6   Correlation r = 0.68

First, the separate standard errors are found:

$$SE_{mA} = \frac{7}{\sqrt{(26-1)}} = \frac{7}{5} = 1.4$$

$$SE_{mB} = \frac{5.6}{\sqrt{(26-1)}} = \frac{5.6}{5} = 1.12$$

In the formula:

$$\begin{aligned}
SE_{diff.AB} &= \sqrt{[(1.4)^2 + (1.12)^2 - 2 \times 0.68 \times 1.4 \times 1.12]} \\
&= \sqrt{(1.96 + 1.25 - 2.13)} \\
&= \sqrt{(3.21 - 2.13)} \\
&= \sqrt{1.08} \\
&= 1.04
\end{aligned}$$

The critical ratio is found by dividing the difference between the test means by the relevant standard error. The difference is 99 − 93 = 6 points.

$$CR = \frac{6}{1.04} = 5.77$$

Interpretation

As this value exceeds 2.787, the value for t at the 1 per cent level of confidence for 25 degrees of freedom, the difference between the results can be accepted as highly significant. Thus, if these were scores from two standardised mathematics tests taken in successive years, it would be reasonable to think that the class as a whole had improved to a higher general standard.

If you have similar data, you might work out the critical ratio and evaluate the difference between the two means. (Remember: if CR is below 1.96, significance does not reach the 5 per cent level; if CR is above 2.58, the 1 per cent level is exceeded.) With 25 or fewer in the class, you will have to find statistical tables for values of t appropriate to the degrees of freedom, that is, number in class minus one $(N - 1)$.

COMPARING TWO SCORES FOR AN INDIVIDUAL

This aspect of handling test scores is extremely important for individual target setting. Regrettably the technical points which need close attention are more frequently ignored than taken into account. Their importance stems from the fact that differences between test scores are relatively more prone to error than either of the originating scores.

Reference back to the section on the SE score for a single test shows that the variability associated with any obtained score is dependent on two factors, that is, the test reliability coefficient and the standard deviation of a score distribution (obtained from a sample of pupils). Clearly, test score differences must take both test reliabilities into account as well as the correlation between pupils' scores. One formula for estimating the reliability of the difference between the two scores, when r_{AB} is the inter-test correlation coefficient, and r_A and r_B as the test reliability coefficients, is

$$r_{\text{diff.AB}} = \frac{r_A + r_B - 2r_{AB}}{2(1 - r_{AB})}$$

To illustrate these factors, suppose we have data as follows: $r_A = 0.9$, $r_B = 0.8$, $r_{AB} = 0.6$. With these quite high reliabilities, and the tests moderately correlated, the formula gives:

$$r_{\text{diff.AB}} = \frac{0.9 + 0.8 - 2 \times 0.6}{2(1 - 0.6)}$$

$$= \frac{1.7 - 1.2}{2 - 1.2} = \frac{0.5}{0.8} = 0.625 \text{ (only a middling value)}$$

The difference reliability coefficient could be used in the formula for an individual score standard error to give the standard error of the difference, but it is really necessary only to understand that score differences tend to be less reliable than the respective parent variables. Another point is that high correlation between two variables gives rise to less reliable differences; any differences that occur are mainly error variations. Consequently, it is necessary to examine correlations between tests for the sample of pupils concerned. However, if only a few pupils are being considered, data from comparable samples will be needed, otherwise sensible estimates of inter-correlations will suffice.

As an approximate guide, if two tests have an average reliability of 0.90 and are correlated at a low level, about 0.30, the difference between scores for interpretation at the 5 per cent level of significance is about the combined standard errors of score. If the average reliability for the tests was around 0.80 and the inter-correlation was about 0.5, the difference at the same level of confidence would be about 1.5 times the combined standard errors.

Usually tests of the same attribute correlate quite highly. So if a pupil is compared on, say, two tests of English given a year apart, relatively small score differences would be regarded as chance variations. Larger differences, say from 0.5 to 1 of the averaged test standard errors, could be regarded as a trend to be noted. Beyond this level larger differences could be interpreted as a marked educational gain or loss.

Profiles

Test manuals for batteries of tests ought to give data which allow the user to see how differences between pairs of test results can be evaluated. One fairly simple way is to provide a set of graphic scales and lay out score sheets which lead the user to mark each pupil's result as a confidence band. An example is given in Figure 11. Here the bands would represent the standard error of score (that is, one standard deviation in estimated distribution of 'true' score). Where the confidence bands overlap, the score differences would be regarded as probably due to chance. Where there is no overlap, differences could be regarded as significant. In this example the A vs B difference would be ignored while the C vs A and C vs B differences would be interpreted.

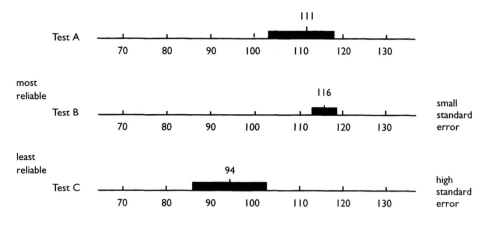

Figure 11 Illustration of profile scores with confidence bands of one standard error

When there are several tests in a 'battery', it is common practice to join score points on a chart as a profile. This procedure tends to overlook the comparison of confidence bands, and it also imposes an order on the results which encourages examining adjacent pairs of results rather than all possible pairs. For example, a battery of six tests gives rise to 5 + 4 + 3 +2 + 1 pairs of results, that is, 15 in all. To illustrate this point, consider a profile for three ability tests and three attainment tests, all scaled to normalised standard scores with a mean of 100 and SD of 15 (Figure 12). The test scores shown are at the mid-point of the confidence bands of ±1SE score.

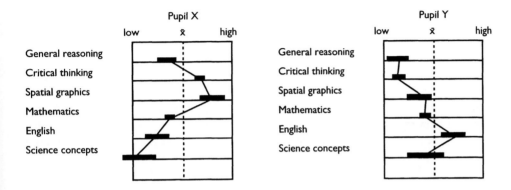

Figure 12 Two graphic profiles compared

This presentation encourages 'at a glance' interpretation along the lines that Pupil X is an under-achiever and Pupil Y is somehow below average in ability and of average attainment (is this an over-achiever?). When interpretation along these lines occurs, there is severe reduction of the meaning available in the data. This happens because

- the order of variables in the list is somewhat arbitrary
- the zigzag of five lines acquires undue importance
- the obtained scores are emphasised, even though the score confidence bands are drawn on the chart.

Profiles can be useful as the uniform presentation of results offers a framework for interpretation. But all of the data should be examined critically, keeping in mind the technical question 'How reliable are the differences which are being compared?'

FOLLOWING UP TEST RESULTS: PREDICTING FROM TEST DATA

It has been said that the best that can be done with educational measures is to derive relevant descriptive statistics. However, a feature of test scores is that their meaning depends, to a large extent, on inference. This is true even for attainment tests which are criterion-referenced, because of the domain sampling which is necessitated (unless only a very restricted domain is assessed or it is treated exhaustively).

To make justifiable inferences it is necessary not only to examine test or assessment specifications (for evidence or assumptions about populations, question domains, judgement bases, content of questions, referencing to criteria and norms), but also to relate the test data to other educational information of concern. For example, an 'attitudes towards technology' questionnaire was designed to assess interest in the field and willingness to study technological applications. Its usefulness for guidance (validity) would be confirmed if significant differences were found between pupils with a technology-loaded curriculum and others with an ordinary curriculum. Evaluating these 'effects' entails looking for association between pupils' experience and their attitudes. In general, investigating association entails examining the relationship between two assessments of the same pupils.

Projecting from Trends over Time: Rolling Means

Treating groups of pupils as samples from a population leads us to expect variations due to chance or circumstances. Some years you may have several outstanding pupils, in others you may have frequent absentees or fewer able children; teaching quality may vary, too. Looking only at yearly variations when setting targets may obscure firm trends. Smoothing fluctuations gives a better basis for making forecasts. You can do this by averaging mean scores for several years and showing these on a chart, as in Figure 13 for reading quotient (RQ) in Year 3 and KS2 English level in Year 6. (Here we know that the SDs were similar in successive years.)

RQ/level	1995		1996		1997		1998		1999
110/80%									
105/75%							106	78	105
100/70%			101	72		73			
95/65%	97				99				
90/60%		62							
	RQ	Eng	RQ	Eng	RQ	Eng	RQ	Eng	RQ

Figure 13 Reading quotient (Year 3) and KS2 English level (Year 6)

The best we can do for the first two years is to average reading quotients and test percentages, to give 99 and 67 per cent respectively. For 95 to 97, the values are 99 and 69 per cent; for 96 to 98 they are 102 and 74.3 per cent; for 97 to 99 RQ average is 103.3 while KS2 for 97 and 98 only is 75.5 per cent. Clearly, the three-year results are the more reliable as they are based on cohorts of 58 to 67 pupils, so the standard errors are halved. Suppose the SDs averaged 12 points for a three-year span, and the total number of pupils was 186, the SE_m would be 12/13.4 = 0.896 and 95 per cent confidence band is ±1.75. These results have been plotted by hand in Figure 14.

Figure 14 shows an optimistic projection for 1999, given that KS2 results for English had tended to improve relative to the earlier RQ assessments. For 1999 we would set a target of 80 per cent even though the RQ mean was only 105 for the group in Year 3. Each of the 'new' means represents an estimate within a band of probable means indicated by the standard error values. For the RQ, you can average the annual SDs and take N as the total number of pupils for the two or three years combined.

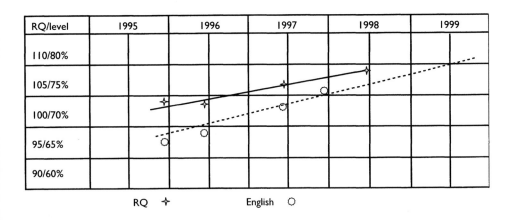

RQ/level	1995	1996	1997	1998	1999
110/80%					
105/75%					
100/70%					
95/65%					
90/60%					

RQ ✛   English ○

Figure 14 Trend lines projected from rolling means

The formula for the standard error of a percentage is given below.

$\dfrac{\sqrt{PQ}}{\sqrt{N}}$ The square root of the product percentage passing criterion, P, and the percentage failing, Q, is divided by N, the group size.

For a target of 80 per cent with a group of 60 pupils, SE_{perc} would be 5.1 per cent. You can see that the 95 per cent confidence band is about 10 per cent. For the rolling mean, the standard error value with aggregated group size of, say, 186 would be 2.9 per cent and the 95 per cent confidence band 74 to 86 per cent. This example shows that forecasting results is not an exact science. The KS English tests may not measure the same attainments year after year, neither do we know their reliabilities, whereas the RQ has a high published reliability coefficient. The target is fine, but there should be a 'court of inquiry' only if the result achieved were outside the confidence band.

Chi-square

Cross-classification may allow you to identify differences between pupil groups which are of concern to the school. The Chi-square (Greek letter χ^2, pronounced 'ky') statistic may be useful for evaluating significance if association is not clearly evident. For example, in a school with 200 pupils in a year-group which has 40 pupils studying a technology-biased curriculum, pupils could be classified simultaneously both ways, that is, above or below the median on an attitude towards technology scale, and in the ordinary curriculum or technology group. The situation that *obtains* can be compared with the situation *expected* if the groups had no difference in attitude. The two-by-two grids exemplify both situations.

		obtained				expected		
		ordinary	technology			ordinary	technology	
Attitude	above	70	30	100	above	80	20	100
scale	below	90	10	100	below	80	20	100
		160	40	200		160	40	200
		Curriculum				Curriculum		

From the numbers of pupils shown in the margins, we can work out how many pupils would be expected in each category cell by calculating the proportion of the total for each cell. For example, the expected number following the ordinary curriculum and above the median attitude score is $100 \times 160 / 200 = 80$. χ^2 is calculated by finding the squared differences between obtained and expected frequencies divided by the expected frequency for each cell and totalling up.

$(O - E)^2/E$

$(-10 \times -10)/80$	$(10 \times 10)/20$
$(10 \times 10)/80$	$(-10 \times -10)/20$

which gives

1.25	5.0
1.25	5.0

totalling 12.5

The null hypothesis implied by the expected frequencies is firmly disproved as the value for χ^2 of 12.5 is almost twice the 1 per cent significance level given in the table. For a two-by-two table, using the rule of rows minus one multiplied by columns minus one, the degrees of freedom are $(2 - 1) \times (2 - 1) = 1$. In other words, there is a very high probability of an association between following the technology curriculum and a more favourable attitude towards technology (research does not always produce this finding), so it would be appropriate to use the scale for pupil guidance.

An association does not necessarily show that one event caused the other, though without an alternative explanation there may be a strong inference. There is a great deal more to using χ^2 than has been indicated here. It offers a sound method for evaluating association between categories of pupil (such as course taken, free school meals, gender, etc.) and measures of attainment. Values of χ^2 at the 95 per cent level of confidence for a range of degrees of freedom (df) are: 1df 3.841, 2df 5.991, 3df 7.815, 4df 9.448, 5df 11.070, 6df 12.592, 7df 14,067, 8df 15.507 and 9df 16.919.

Correlation
Pupils can also be cross-classified according to their scores on a pair of tests (or other measures) to produce a joint frequency distribution.

Figure 15 shows the results from a sample of pupils in an LEA given oral language tests and several writing tasks, with both marked in raw scores up to a maximum of 55. The results are plotted on a grid with five-point class intervals. Each tally mark stands for an individual pupil's results (some computer plots will not show the number of pupils in each cell of the plot, so some hand plotting may be useful). We can see, for example, that one pupil obtained only a score below 5 for each test, while two pupils scored between 36 and 40 for written English but came between 6 and 10 for oral.

Computers handle the extensive arithmetic entailed in an instant. However, it is useful to picture the scatter in relation to the size of the coefficient of correlation. In the plot illustrated all but a few pupils' results could be enclosed in a 'fat cigar' shape. If the tallies are concentrated densely along the leading diagonal, the correlation coefficient is very high, between 0.9 and 1.0. In this case it is possible to talk *in future of* predicting fairly accurately pupils' scores on the y-variable from the x-variable score. When the degree of correlation is lower, it is still possible to predict a y score but with less confidence. The two diagrams in Figure 16 show why.

On each diagram the sloping straight line runs close to the mid-points of the vertical lines drawn through the crosses showing individual plots for x and y scores.

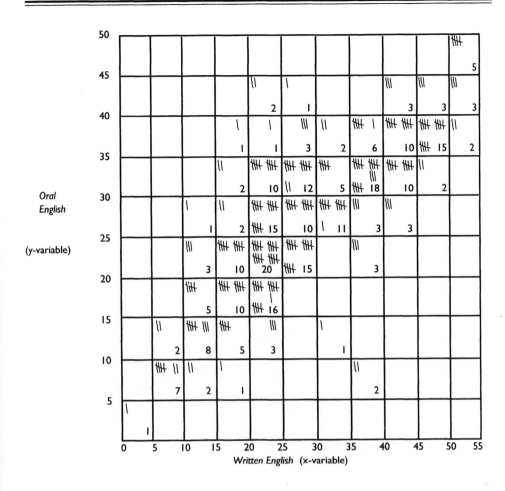

Figure 15 Scattergram of bi-variate distribution (N = 282)

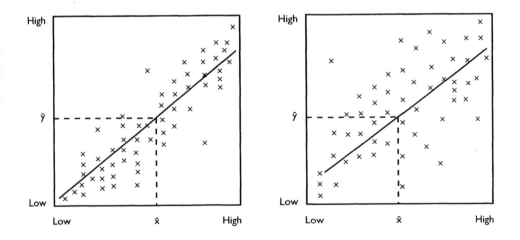

Figure 16 Regression lines on bi-variate distributions for 'high' and 'moderate' correlations

In fact the vertical lines show the range and distribution of y scores corresponding to any x score. The high correlation regression line approaches an angle of 45, whereas the lower correlation *regression* line has a shallower angle; for zero correlation the line would be horizontal. Although a score on variable y can be estimated from any given value of x, the confidence band associated with y (derived from the *standard error of estimated score*) will be much wider for lower values of the coefficient.

Computer regression plots usually show only the line for variable y scores 'predicted' from the x variable. However, x can be 'predicted' from y, for which a *second* regression line would be drawn. This line would make the same angle to the y-axis as the x on y regression line makes to the x-axis. The two lines intersect at the mean values for both of the variables. Most computer programs will produce scatter diagrams and only the x on y regression line. One or more pupils with the same pair of scores appear as one spot on the plot (so you may wish to check through individual scores to record the numbers manually) and it is unlikely that the plot will be shown in cells (so these may have to be drawn manually, if required).

There is a widespread notion that many tests can be used to predict a pupil's potential for scholastic attainment. The two points to appreciate are, first, that the prediction is necessarily based on the correlation obtained for pupils in another, earlier, sample – which is then generalised to other samples; second, that very high correlations between the test and the measure of achievement would be needed to predict confidently for any given pupil. A glance at the right-hand diagram in Figure 16 explains why. A pupil with a score of x (remember this can be any score on variable x) may turn out to be in any of the positions plotted on the vertical line in the scatter plot.

An estimated y score can be computed from the *regression equation* for each of the values of x. The standard error of this Y_E given is the SD of the y variable obtained from a previous sample:

$$Y_E = \bar{y} + r_{x,y} \times \frac{SD_y}{SD_x} (x - \bar{x})$$

Estimated score is mean for variable y plus individual's x deviation score multiplied by the product of the correlation coefficient and the ratio of the SDs.

Notes

The estimated score, Y_E, depends on the assumption that the regression lines, would be straight, a condition known as 'linearity'. If the scatter is 'banana shaped', prediction should be treated with caution. Prediction can be done for selection test score, x, which is used to find a probable criterion score, YE, using values from previous sample data. This method is acceptable only if the mean for x, the SD and correlation have been consistent on previous occasions.

The standard error of predicted scores is greater than either the standard error of the predictor variable, x, or original criterion variable, y. Test manuals which discuss prediction should give the data necessary for a user to gauge the size of the standard error of estimated score. Tests of ability or aptitude are often said to predict future performance. You can see that prediction is seldom precise and that even high correlations between a predictor and criterion can give only approximate indicators for any further predictions.

Residuals

Whenever correlation is less than perfect, a number of the data points for individual pupils or classes or schools will plot at some distance from the regression line. You see these in the vertical crosses above and below the line in Figure 16. These distances represent the 'unexplained' or residual variation from the general trend shown in the relationship between x and y. The values of residuals are sometimes treated as indicators of untoward discrepancies rather than the 'unexplained variation' (the sum of vertical distances of points above the line equals the sum of distances for points below the line), in particular of under-performance in 'value added' analyses. In such instances, schools are asked to look for reasons why they are not in line with the others, or individual pupils may be shown they have much to do to come up to expectation.

Standard errors can be computed for the range of residual values and these are usually given at the 95 per cent level of confidence. Several value added schemes use 'multi-level' analyses, which employ measures of differing kinds, of schools and individuals (e.g. ethnicity, free school meals, screening test scores, pupil–teacher ratio) and these will generally explain more of the relative variation between schools than a regression analysis carried out with two or more variables of the same kind. Again, the assumption is made that schools falling outside the confidence band have some explaining to do. In fact, the scheme may not include information of crucial importance to schools with lower attainment levels, such as the proportion of pupils on the SEN register.

Expectancy Tables

You may wish to give pupils guidance or set targets in a less technical way than using a regression equation. Imagine that the predicted outcome is external examination success and the predictor variable is a standardised test of reasoning ability. With data from previous cohorts of pupils, taking GCSE grades as the criterion in a given subject and dividing the reasoning test score range, of say 85 to 140, into eight bands of seven points, gives a scatter diagram as shown in Figure 17.

The numbers in each cell show how pupils tested in the second year fared in the fifth-year examination in mathematics. There is an obvious correlation between the prior ability assessment and subsequent mathematics examination. But for purposes of guidance it is more useful to calculate the expected outcome under the assumption that successive groups of pupils will obtain closely comparable results. You simply need to calculate the percentage likelihood of obtaining a particular grade for a corresponding test score. As Figure 17 shows, there are a large number of cells with small numbers and it is preferable to merge adjacent cells into broader categories. If these have an educational import, so much the better. Say that a school has to decide whether to enter pupils for a high-level GCSE assessment awarding A and B grades, then combining pairs of grades seems to be sensible. It also simplifies matters to combine adjacent reasoning score columns, as shown in Figure 18.

With an accumulated series of results from successive years, the table could be drawn up in the original eight-by-eight format. As it stands, the expectation of obtaining either grades A or B is lower than the expectation of obtaining grades C or D for pupils whose test scores were over 126. The only way to verify whether expectancy tables can be helpful tools is to get the data and do the tabulations. In

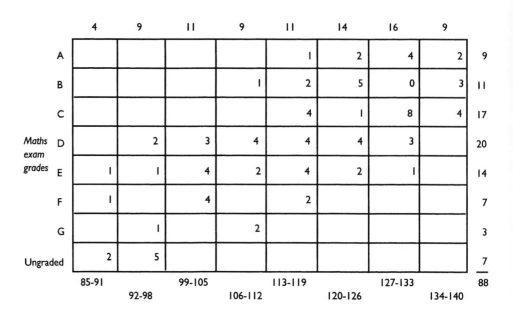

	4	9	11	9	11	14	16	9	
A					1	2	4	2	9
B				1	2	5	0	3	11
C					4	1	8	4	17
D		2	3	4	4	4	3		20
E	1	1	4	2	4	2	1		14
F	1		4		2				7
G		1		2					3
Ungraded	2	5							7
	85-91	92-98	99-105	106-112	113-119	120-126	127-133	134-140	88

Maths exam grades (row label)

Figure 17 Example of expectancy table

Test score

Grades	85-98	99-112	113-126	127-140
A and B		1 5%	10 32%	9 39%
C and D	2 15%	7 35%	13 42%	15 65%
E and F	3 23%	10 50%	8 26%	1 4%
G and Ungraded	8 62%	2 10%		
	13	20	31	23

For this cell $\frac{15}{23} = 65\%$

Figure 18 Expected grades from test scores

addition, if tables are drawn up for different subjects, the utility of particular predictor variables can be evaluated.

It is worth pointing out that a great deal of 'prediction' goes on in education, though often it is not recognised as such. Examples are setting; banding; restricted options; allocation to special education groups; access to exceptional pupils' opportunities; entry for limited grade examinations; matching pupils with the appropriate Key Stage test; and, less specifically, forecasts of progress and potential (targets) in comments and reports.

Making Complex Inferences

The heading implies that the inferences described previously are not complex. This is not really the case, but when a range of data can be obtained from tests and other sources, it may be useful for teachers or the school to examine the extent to which variables interrelate, and to interpret the results inferentially. Imagine that there are variables A, B, C, D, E, F and G; these are paired in succession to give the correlation of A with B, A with C, A with D, and so on. As the coefficient for AvsB is the same as for BvsA, and so on, it is necessary only to display inter-correlations for a set of variables in a minimal format. For example, a test manual could show the correlations for various sub-tests with the other sub-tests and teachers' ratings as in Figure 19.

	Sp.	Voc.	Syn.	Comp.	Fl.	Ess.	Disc.	Poe.
Spelling	–	0.8	0.7	0.5	0.6	0.8	0.5	0.2
Vocabulary		–	0.6	0.8	0.8	0.8	0.6	0.8
Syntax			–	0.7	0.4	0.7	0.2	–0.4
Comprehension				–	0.5	0.5	0.4	0.6
Fluency					–	0.7	0.6	0.3
TR Essays						–	0.3	0.4
TR Discussion							–	0.3
TR Poetry								–

Figure 19 Inter-correlations between sub-skills and teachers' ratings of progress

Significance levels are determined according to the sample size, by referring to the appropriate statistical table. Some computer programs incorporate the tables, and print-outs indicate conventional levels, at 5 per cent and 1 per cent, usually by printing a single or a double asterisk respectively alongside the relevant coefficient.

The high to moderate values shown in the example are typical when variables which measure activities in the same curriculum area are correlated. However, had these figures come from a sample as small as ten pupils, only values over 0.6 would be significant at or beyond the 5 per cent level of significance. For a group of about 30 the value falls to almost 0.35, while for a group of about 100 the value is almost 0.20. In fact, though groups of pupils in particular schools would not have the same characteristics as groups chosen at random from the population (because their social background and school experiences tend to make for similarities within the group), it is nevertheless helpful to examine the significance levels for the given sample size.

Another way in which inter-correlations can be used is in multiple correlations, symbolised by R. Using the previous example, one question might be 'To what extent is essay writing related to vocabulary and syntax when combined together?' In the jargon the essay score is the criterion (or dependent variable), while the language test sub-scores are the predictors (or independent variables). To find R it is easier to find R^2 then to take the square root. Treating the essay score as variable 1, with the vocabulary and syntax scores as variables 2 and 3 respectively, the formula for R^2 is:

$$R^2_{1.23} = \frac{r^2_{12} + r^2_{13} - 2r_{12}\,r_{13}\,r_{23}}{1 - r^2_{23}}$$

Substituting values from the matrix in Figure 19, we have

$$R^2_{1.23} = \frac{0.8^2 + 0.7^2 - 2 \times 0.8 \times 0.7 \times 0.6}{1 - 0.6^2}$$

$$= \frac{0.64 + 0.49 - 0.672}{1 - 0.36}$$

$$= \frac{1.13 - 0.672}{0.64}$$

so $$R^2 = \frac{0.458}{0.64} = 0.72$$

hence $R = 0.85$.

The increase in association between the criterion and separate predictors is quite marked. It is unlikely, though, that adding more variables to the equation would greatly enhance the degree of relationship. The reason is that, in this case, the predictor variables overlap with each other considerably, as shown by the correlation coefficients of 0.5 and over. Compared with bi-variate regression, in which an estimated Y_E score is obtained from a given x score, multiple regression uses the results from a number of predictor variables, x_1, x_2, $x_3 \dots x_n$ to produce the estimate Y_E. The multiple regression equation has 'weights' which are coefficients applied to each pupil's predictor variable scores. Trial samples provide these data, and also a value for R^2. Expressed as a percentage (as with r^2) the value shows how much of the joint variation was accounted for by the combined variables (for the group of pupils studied). The nearer R^2 is to 100 per cent, the more efficient the equation. In general, multiple regression equations should be taken seriously only if the value for R^2 is in excess of 60 per cent.

Incidentally the fabricated inter-correlation matrix shown above incorporates some features which test users should look out for. One is that the sub-tests tend to correlate highly, partly because test structures tap similar attributes (some children enjoy a test and so do well, others sink dismally). A batch of high inter-correlations also shows that the sub-tests are not neatly differentiating between attributes. When reading test manuals for evidence of validity, you should look for high correlations with criteria which interest you and give less weight to coefficients showing relationships with other, similar tests or between sub-tests.

Appendix 1

SAMPLE DATA FOR TWO CLASSES WITH 68 PUPILS – BOYS (TABLE 16)

Table 16 Sample data for two classes with 68 pupils – boys (Pupil performance on Writing Test/Task)

Surname	First name	Sex	Nurs	FSM	Write T/T		Maths T/T		ScSubLvl
Adams	John	b	Yes	Yes	2C		2C		2
Andrews	Geoffrey	b	Yes	No	2B		2A		3
Bennet	Peter	b	Yes	No		3		3	3
Bowen	Peter	b	Yes	No		3		3	3
Brain	Richard	b	Yes	No	2C		2A		3
Brown	John	b	Yes	No	2C		2B		2
Burton	Alistair	b	Yes	No	2B			3	3
Burton	Reg	b	No	No		3		3	3
Cane	Sean	b	Yes	No	2C		2A		3
Clegg	Oliver	b	Yes	No	2B			3	3
Collin	David	b	Yes	No	2C		2C		2
Curtis	Harold	b	Yes	No		2	2C		2
Dunne	William	b	Yes	No	2B		2A		2
English	Leonard	b	Yes	No	2A		2B		3
French	Ian	b	Yes	No		3		3	3
Godfrey	Sam	b	Yes	No		2	2C		2
Green	John	b	Yes	No	2B			3	3
Hall	Wain	b	Yes	No	2C		2C		1
Howard	Arthur	b	No	Yes	2C		2B		2
Howe	Gordon	b	Yes	Yes	2C		2C		2
Jones	Andrew	b	No	No	2B			3	3
Katlin	Earnest	b	Yes	No	2C		2B		2
Macrae	Neil	b	Yes	No		2		2	1
Noble	Dennis	b	No	No	2C		2B		2

Table 16 Continued

Surname	First name	Sex	Nurs	FSM	Write T/T	Maths T/T	ScSubLvl
Reed	Stephen	b	No	Yes	2B	2A	2
Spencer	Ian	b	No	No	2C	2	2
Staples	Seamus	b	Yes	No	2C	2C	2
Street	Neil	b	No	No	3	3	3
Thorpe	Alan	b	Yes	No	2B	2B	3
Vernon	Charles	b	No	No	2B	2A	3
Ward	Roger	b	Yes	No	2A	3	3
Weston	Colin	b	No	No	2B	3	3
White	Gerald	b	Yes	No	2C	2A	3
Wood	Donald	b	Yes	No	2A	3	3

Key   Nurs   attended nursery provision
       FSM   has free school meals
       Write T/T   Key Stage 1 Test or Task level attained in writing
       Maths T/T   Key Stage 1 Test or Task level attained in maths
       ScSubLvl   Key Stage subject level attained in science

SAMPLE DATA FOR TWO CLASSES WITH 68 PUPILS – GIRLS (TABLE 17)

Table 17 Sample data for two classes with 68 pupils – girls

Surname	First name	Sex	Nurs	FSM	Write T/T	Maths T/T	ScSubLvl
Courtney	Mary	g	Yes	No	3	3	3
Couzens	Joan	g	Yes	Yes	2B	3	2
Coward	Hilary	g	No	No	2C	3	3
Crick	Susan	g	Yes	No	2A	2A	3
Crombie	Jane	g	Yes	No	2B	3	2
Dee	Sarah	g	Yes	No	2B	3	2
Dowding	Lorna	g	Yes	No	2B	2B	2
Haydock	Liza	g	Yes	No	2C	2B	2
Haynes	Lynda	g	Yes	No	2B	2B	3
Johnson	Yvonne	g	Yes	No	2C	2B	2
Lawrence	Kate	g	No	Yes	2C	2A	2
Macrae	Jean	g	Yes	No	2A	2A	2
Pollard	Jennifer	g	Yes	No	2C	2C	1
Poole	Elizabeth	g	Yes	Yes	2C	2C	2
Rutherford	Catherine	g	Yes	No	2C	2C	2
Saggers	June	g	Yes	No	2A	2A	3
Tate	Mary	g	No	No	2B	3	3
Taylor	Colleen	g	Yes	No	2C	2C	2
Tennison	Alison	g	Yes	No	2A	2B	3
Tyrrell	Nancy	g	Yes	No	2C	2	2
Upton	Leslie	g	Yes	No	2B	3	3
Vander	Janet	g	Yes	No	2A	2A	3
Walsh	Elizabeth	g	Yes	No	2B	2A	2
Watts	Sandra	g	Yes	No	2B	3	3

Table 17 Continued

Surname	First name	Sex	Nurs	FSM	Write T/T		Maths T/T		ScSubLvl
Weaver	Sylvia	g	Yes	Yes	2C		2C		2
Webb	Susan	g	Yes	No		3		3	3
Weeks	Hazel	g	Yes	No		3		3	3
Weller	Wendy	g	Yes	No	2C		2B		2
Whelan	Wendy	g	Yes	No		3	2A		3
Williams	Martha	g	Yes	No	2B			3	3
Williams	Sarah	g	No	No	2C		2B		2
Woodside	Julia	g	Yes	No	2B		2A		3
Wortley	Beryl	g	Yes	No	2C		2B		2
Young	Megan	g	Yes	No	2A			3	3

Appendix 2

Tables 18 and 19 contain information relating to Key Stage 1 pupils. Data for each pupil have been coded as follows: Sex: Boys – 1; Girls – 2. Nurs: Pupils who attended nursery school – 1; others – 2. FSM: Pupils eligible for free school meals – 1; others – 2. WriteT/T (Writing Test/Task performance) and MathsT/T (Mathematics Test/Task performance) Levels 3 – 3; A – 2.75; B – 2.5; C – 2.25; 1 – 2; W – 1.5. ScSubLvl (science subject level) grades as recorded.

SAMPLE DATA FOR TWO CLASSES WITH 68 PUPILS – BOYS (NUMERIC CODES)

Table 18 Sample data for two classes with 68 pupils – boys (numeric codes)

Surname	First name	Sex	Nurs	FSM	Write T/T	Maths T/T	ScSubLvl
Adams	John	1	1	1	2.25	2.25	2
Andrews	Geoffrey	1	1	2	2.5	2.75	3
Bennet	Peter	1	1	2	3	3	3
Bowen	Peter	1	1	2	3	3	3
Brain	Richard	1	1	2	2.25	2.75	3
Brown	John	1	1	2	2.25	2.5	2
Burton	Alistair	1	1	2	2.5	3	3
Burton	Reg	1	2	2	3	3	3
Cane	Sean	1	1	2	2.25	2.75	3
Clegg	Oliver	1	1	2	2.5	3	3
Collin	David	1	1	2	2.25	2.25	2
Curtis	Harold	1	1	2	2	2.25	2
Dunne	William	1	1	2	2.5	2.75	2
English	Leonard	1	1	2	2.75	2.5	3
French	Ian	1	1	2	3	3	3
Godfrey	Sam	1	1	2	2	2.25	2
Green	John	1	1	2	2.5	3	3
Hall	Wain	1	1	2	2.25	2.25	1
Howard	Arthur	1	2	1	2.25	2.5	2

Table 18 Continued

Surname	First name	Sex	Nurs	FSM	Write T/T	Maths T/T	ScSubLvl
Howe	Gordon	1	1	1	2.25	2.25	2
Jones	Andrew	1	2	2	2.5	3	3
Katlin	Earnest	1	1	2	2.25	2.5	2
Macrae	Neil	1	1	2	2	2	1
Noble	Dennis	1	2	2	2.25	2.5	2
Reed	Stephen	1	2	1	2.5	2.75	2
Spencer	Ian	1	2	2	2.25	2	2
Staples	Seamus	1	1	2	2.25	2.25	2
Street	Neil	1	2	2	3	3	3
Thorpe	Alan	1	1	2	2.5	2.5	3
Vernon	Charles	1	2	2	2.5	2.75	3
Ward	Roger	1	1	2	2.75	3	3
Weston	Colin	1	2	2	2.5	3	3
White	Gerald	1	1	2	2.25	2.75	3
Wood	Donald	1	1	2	2.75	3	3

SAMPLE DATA FOR TWO CLASSES WITH 68 PUPILS
– GIRLS (NUMERIC CODES)

Table 19 Sample data for two classes with 68 pupils – girls (numeric codes)

Surname	First name	Sex	Nurs	FSM	Write T/T	Maths T/T	ScSubLvl
Courtney	Mary	2	1	2	3	3	3
Couzens	Joan	2	1	1	2.5	3	2
Coward	Hilary	2	2	2	2.25	3	3
Crick	Susan	2	1	2	2.75	2.75	3
Crombie	Jane	2	1	2	2.5	3	2
Dee	Sarah	2	1	2	2.5	3	2
Dowding	Lorna	2	1	2	2.5	2.5	2
Haydock	Liza	2	1	2	2.25	2.5	2
Haynes	Lynda	2	1	2	2.5	2.5	3
Johnson	Yvonne	2	1	2	2.25	2.5	2
Lawrence	Kate	2	2	1	2.25	2.75	2
Macrae	Jean	2	1	2	2.75	2.75	2
Pollard	Jennifer	2	1	2	2.25	2.25	1
Poole	Elizabeth	2	1	1	2.25	2.25	2
Rutherford	Catherine	2	1	2	2.25	2.25	2
Saggers	June	2	1	2	2.75	2.75	3
Tate	Mary	2	2	2	2.5	3	3
Taylor	Colleen	2	1	2	2.25	2.25	2
Tennison	Alison	2	1	2	2.75	2.5	3
Tyrrell	Nancy	2	1	2	2.25	2	2
Upton	Leslie	2	1	2	2.5	3	3
Vander	Janet	2	1	2	2.75	2.75	3
Walsh	Elizabeth	2	1	2	2.5	2.75	2
Watts	Sandra	2	1	2	2.5	3	3

Table 19 Continued

Surname	First name	Sex	Nurs	FSM	Write T/T	Maths T/T	ScSubLvl
Weaver	Sylvia	2	1	1	2.25	2.25	2
Webb	Susan	2	1	2	3	3	3
Weeks	Hazel	2	1	2	3	3	3
Weller	Wendy	2	1	2	2.25	2.5	2
Whelan	Wendy	2	1	2	3	2.75	3
Williams	Martha	2	1	2	2.5	3	3
Williams	Sarah	2	2	2	2.25	2.5	2
Woodside	Julia	2	1	2	2.5	2.75	3
Wortley	Beryl	2	1	2	2.25	2.5	2
Young	Megan	2	1	2	2.75	3	3

Appendix 3

RECEPTION PUPIL PERFORMANCE AND
CONTEXTUAL DATA FROM 61 SCHOOLS

Table 20 contains information derived from pupils in reception classes in 61 schools located in a single local education authority. In order to ensure that no school could be identified, actual school names have been changed with randomly selected names and the data reordered.

A description of the variables recorded for each school is provided below. Those numbered between 7 and 11 were derived from the Census and are the mean proportions of persons in the enumeration districts in which pupils' homes are located.

Col.
1 A number used to identify each school
2 Reading   mean scores on a test of reading
3 Writing   mean scores on a test of writing
4 Speaking   mean scores on an assessment of speaking
5 Maths   mean scores on a test of mathematics
6 FSM   proportion of pupils eligible for free school meals
7 Soc. Class. proportions of persons aged 16+ who are managers/ administrators or professional
8 Qual.   proportions of adults aged 18+ with qualifications at level of diploma or above
9 Unempl.   unemployed persons as proportion of the 'economically active'
10 Overcrowd   proportion of households with one or more persons per room

Table 20

	School	Reading	Writing	Speaking	Maths	FSM	Soc.Cl.	Qual.	Unempl.	Overc'd
1	Abbey Court School	4.26	1.72	1.56	3.3	0.6	24.22	5.97	13.92	4.45
2	Abbey School	4.73	1.84	2.11	3.17	0.53	14.8	10.7	22.53	5.96
3	Archers Court School	4.56	1.76	1.33	3.53	0.13	38.58	29.2	7.87	2.35
4	Ashton School	5.51	2.42	1.11	4	0.04	19.93	9.33	8.5	4.32
5	Astor School	3.33	1.59	1.04	2.37	0.39	20.81	8.06	12.67	4.12
6	Beechwood School	4.49	1.93	2.33	2.86	0.28	33.61	31.1	9.96	3.44
7	Bethany School	4.3	2.21	2	3.07	0.16	22.95	6.03	9.88	4.02
8	Bourne Place School	3.82	1.82	1.41	3.55	0.38	19.09	9.76	10.69	5.2
9	Bower Grove School	3.18	1.28	1.31	2.41	0.76	22.69	10.6	17.98	4.41
10	Bradfields School	3.54	1.55	0.95	2.66	0.13	13.46	8.28	18.91	15.74
11	Brockhill Park School	5.25	1.5	0.5	3.5	0.5	32.1	16.9	8.63	1.71
12	Broomhill Bank School	4.66	2.18	1.75	3.57	0.18	22.42	11.3	9.1	3.84
13	Castle Primary School	4.01	1.71	1.86	2.59	0.36	18.03	7.71	10.55	4.91
14	Christ Church CofE Primary	4.73	2.6	1.53	3.69	0.16	25.25	15	16.5	6.29
15	Cobham Lane School	3.1	1.57	0.96	3.62	0.42	28.22	21.5	14.01	5.32
16	Combe Bank School	2.92	1.17	1.46	2.59	0.17	14.63	7.32	15.43	12.43
17	Fineden School	3.66	1.72	1.47	3.53	0.25	24.98	14.2	9.81	3.88
18	Five Acre Wood School	4.9	2.34	2.5	3.93	0.06	37.7	26.3	9.58	3.49
19	Grade Hill School	4.42	1.68	1.32	3.06	0.52	11.17	5.91	14.46	7.07
20	Greystones School	4.8	1.73	1.53	3.82	0.18	27.87	20.7	12.66	4.93
21	Hartsdown Junior School	4.21	2.2	1.55	2.89	0.16	42.13	32.5	7.88	2.39
22	Hayes School	2.71	1.39	1.68	2.86	0.32	30.63	13.3	13.71	5.29
23	Highsted Primary School	5.42	2.47	1.76	3.98	0.16	31.53	19.3	10.84	3.57
24	Highview School	4.35	1.69	1.92	3.47	0.06	38.16	25.3	8.26	1.95
25	Highworth JMI School	4.41	1.28	1.28	2.94	0.16	36.89	24	8.2	2.46
26	Hillview School	3.98	2.1	1.51	3.57	0.15	15.95	5.22	10.23	4.45
27	Holmesdale School	5.05	2.59	2.08	3.59	0.21	22.92	11.6	8.62	3.96
28	Homewood School	4.51	2.22	2.08	3.21	0.11	29.2	16.4	8.98	5.02
29	Longfield Primary School	5.49	2.16	2.12	3.78	0.01	39.63	26.6	7.08	1.61
30	Malting School	4.6	1.98	1.31	3.24	0.14	19.56	15.2	11.16	3.38
31	Meadows School	2.21	0.95	0.48	2.11	0.32	15.68	6.31	14.05	12.06

32	Northfleet Junior School	3.23	2.08	0.78	3.6	0.17	22.22	9.87	11.47	4.68
33	Northway Primary School	4.22	1.84	1.64	2.89	0.16	24.3	13.5	10.07	6.18
34	Oak Bank School	2.75	1.4	1.5	1.85	0.31	13.35	6.07	15.38	14.75
35	Oakwood Park School	4.15	1.93	0.87	2.38	0.33	21.26	10.5	11.17	8.13
36	Orchard School	3.57	1.51	1.19	2.78	0.49	31.54	22.1	16.28	5.75
37	Parkfield School	4.46	2.17	1.54	3.28	0.19	32.79	23.3	12.14	3.45
38	Queen Elizabeth's School	4.51	1.8	1.76	3.27	0.24	15.27	7.57	14.01	9.59
39	Ridge View School	3.74	1.57	1.03	3.09	0.19	18.05	8.66	13.18	6.84
40	Riverside School	5.75	2.59	2.59	5.1	0.02	40.33	32	7.62	2.27
41	Rowhill School	4.81	2.1	1.66	3.49	0.15	29.15	16.4	11.1	4.38
42	Sir John Fuller School	4	2.01	1.01	3.01	0.21	22.74	12.2	10.62	7.37
43	Southfields Primary School	1.68	1.32	0.76	1.08	0.16	15.12	10.9	17.06	12.4
44	St Anthony's School	3.85	2.17	1.22	2.75	0.1	33.99	22.2	9.55	3.81
45	St Augustine's School	4	1.92	2.13	3.35	0.17	13.87	9.61	16.13	13.83
46	St Bartholomew's School	4.08	1.78	2.06	3.2	0.18	16.82	7.51	13.84	11.77
47	St George's CofE School	4.4	2.23	1.37	3.58	0.07	44.42	34.5	5.46	1.52
48	St George's School	2.34	1.6	0.93	2.92	0.22	14.71	8.46	13.46	10.4
49	St John's Primary School	3.87	2.35	2	3.42	0.39	29.09	16.4	11.63	6.17
50	St Lawrence School	2.72	1.38	1.22	2.15	0.24	13.12	5.57	18.83	14.27
51	St Mary's College	4.95	2.34	2.36	4.53	0.14	28.96	19.5	12.65	3.79
52	St Thomas' School	4.03	1.76	1.1	2.9	0.14	25.5	17.7	10.63	3.73
53	Thamesway School	3.36	1.58	0.75	2.94	0.33	13.58	6.73	15.3	5.3
54	The Cedars School	3.57	1.55	1.84	3.07	0.46	20.98	11.5	10.08	4.13
55	The Charles Dickens School	1.85	0.96	0.69	1.42	0.27	9.32	6.43	20.36	19.81
56	The Howard Green School	5.03	2.03	1.89	3.61	0.61	26	13.4	21.21	4.8
57	The Robert Napier School	2.41	1.36	0.32	1.51	0.33	12.57	6.15	18.44	14.68
58	The South Woodlands School	4.85	1.88	0.88	3.5	0.1	20.64	12.4	9.94	3.73
59	The Valley School	3.92	2.03	1.59	3.19	0.3	16.26	7.55	17.64	11.47
60	West Heath School	3.05	1.94	1.52	2.05	0.15	11.7	6.03	17.89	18.53
61	Westlands School	3.31	1.5	1.87	3.25	0.31	22.9	12.1	11.73	7.08

Index